Living in Christ

Vocations

Answering God's Call

Jenna M. Cooper

with Fr. Luke Sweeney and Joanna Dailey

saint mary's press

The Subcommittee on the Catechism, United States Conference of Catholic Bishops, has found that this catechetical high school text, copyright 2013, is in conformity with the *Catechism of the Catholic Church* and that it fulfills the requirements of Elective Course option D: "Responding to the Call of Jesus Christ" of the *Doctrinal Elements of a Curriculum Framework for the Development of Catechetical Materials for Young People of High School Age.*

Nihil Obstat: Rev. William M. Becker, STD
                Censor Librorum
                November 30, 2012
Imprimatur: † Most Rev. John M. Quinn, DD
                Bishop of Winona
                November 30, 2012
The nihil obstat and imprimatur are official declarations that a book or pamphlet is free of doctrinal or moral error. No implication is contained therein that those who have granted the nihil obstat or imprimatur agree with the contents, opinions, or statements expressed, nor do they assume any legal responsibility associated with publication.

The publishing team included Gloria Shahin, editorial director; Steven Ellair, editor; and Maura Thompson Hagarty, PhD, theological reviewer. Prepress and manufacturing coordinated by the production departments of Saint Mary's Press.

The publisher also wishes to thank the following individuals who advised the publishing team or reviewed the work in progress:
Barbara Stanley, MA
Fr. David L. Toups, STD

Printed in the United States of America

1155 (PO5941)

ISBN 978-1-59982-150-4, Print

Contents

Section 1: Living Our Christian Vocation

Section 2: Married Life

Section 3: Ordained Life

Section 4: Consecrated Life

Section 5: Discerning God's Will

Introduction

When you were a young child, you probably frequently heard the question, What do you want to be when you grow up? You have probably continued to answer that question—in one form or another—throughout your school years. Of course, as you have matured, your answer has become more introspective and based on a deeper understanding of your gifts, talents, and interests and of how God may be calling you to use them.

Still, for each of us, finding out who we are and what God is calling us to is an ongoing process of discovery, and as you contemplate life beyond high school, you are probably continuing to ponder important questions: Who am I? What gifts and talents have I been given? What might be my work in the world? What is God calling me to?

You are not alone in facing these questions. You are supported by all of the members of the Church as you figure out how to best respond to God's call in your life. Your faith, your gifts, and your vocation are essential to the life and mission of the Church. You should also be comforted to know that the Holy Spirit is with you, guiding you as you discern your vocation—how God is calling you to serve him and others in the world.

Your participation in the life of the Church will also help you to discern your vocation and achieve your God-given potential. Through daily prayer, reading Sacred Scripture, participating in the Sacraments, learning more about the Church's teachings, reading the accounts of the saints' lives, and seeking advice from caring people in your life, you will learn how to discover the desires of your heart in conversation with God.

As you continue your discernment, this book will help you to learn about the Christian vocation in general and about the vocational states of life: married life, ordained life, consecrated life, and single life. Our hope is that this book will become more than just an informational resource used in an academic course, and that, by learning and reflecting on the material presented here, you will have an opportunity to more deeply engage in the important process of discovering and understanding how God is calling you.

Blessings on your journey of discovery. May we all encourage one another along the way!

The Editors at Saint Mary's Press

Living Our Christian Vocation

Part 1

We Are Called by God

"In the beginning was the Word" (John 1:1), and from the beginning that Word has called to humankind. It is the Word of God that called to us finally and most clearly through the Second Person of the Holy Trinity, Jesus Christ. This is truly Good News—that God is calling us, seeking us, and that we need only to hear and to respond. To respond is to find our life calling, our vocation.

Yet we, as individuals, are not alone in that response. In the first part of this book on vocations, we recall the lives of some who have gone before us, some who have heard God's Word in the midst of their lives and have responded with all their hearts. In the Old Testament, we consider God's call to Abraham, Samuel, Jeremiah, and David. In the New Testament, we examine God's call to Mary, Nathanael, Peter, and Mary Magdalene. All heard, all responded, but each in a very different way.

This gives us hope. We do not all follow Christ in the same way. What is important is that we listen to the voice of the One who knows us, loves us, and asks only that we follow him along the path of life that will lead us to communion with him.

The articles in this part address the following topics:

Article 1 What Is a Vocation?

vocation
A call from God to all members of the Church to embrace a life of holiness. Specifically, it refers to a call to live the holy life as an ordained minister, as a vowed religious (sister or brother), or in a Christian marriage. Single life that involves a personal consecration or commitment to a permanent, celibate gift of self to God and one's neighbor is also a vocational state.

A **vocation** is a gift of grace that God gives to each one of us. The grace of a vocation is the living water of the Holy Spirit that flows from deep within us, giving us life and purpose. It is a personal call from God to embrace a certain way of life, a way of life that will enable us to use all our gifts and talents to serve him and one another. A vocation is a call from God, but it requires a response on our part. Both the call and the response are pure gift. We are assisted by God's grace in discerning and living our vocation.

To understand this gift of vocation, we need to think of it in the widest possible context. The word *vocation* has special meaning in the life of the Church. First and foremost, it refers to the foundational call from God, which is the call to holiness and communion with him. But it also refers to the different states of life through which we are called, in a particular way, to live out our foundational vocation. These vocational states of life include married life, consecrated life, and ordained life. Single life that involves a personal consecration or commitment to a permanent, celibate gift of self to God and one's neighbor is also a vocational state. We will look at each of these states of life in more detail throughout this book.

Although the term *vocation* is sometimes used for a career or a job (as in "vocational training"), it has a far deeper meaning in our life as Christians. The work we do every day (even if we do not consider it a career) is important. It too is a gift from God because it helps us to grow and to serve others. But careers, jobs, and everyday tasks are changeable and are usually part of a wider and deeper vocation, the fulfillment of which is eternal happiness with God in Heaven.

A vocation is a personal call from God that springs forth from deep within us. In order to begin to discover your vocation, it can be helpful to reflect on those things you value as important, meaningful, and life-giving.

© Maxim Tupikov/Shutterstock.com

Tradition

This word (from the Latin, meaning "to hand on") refers to the process of passing on the Gospel message. Tradition, which began with the oral communication of the Gospel by the Apostles, was written down in Scripture, is handed down and lived out in the life of the Church, and is interpreted by the Magisterium under the guidance of the Holy Spirit.

Longing for God

"You have made us for yourself, O Lord, and our hearts are restless until they rest in you." This famous quotation from Saint Augustine of Hippo perfectly expresses the relationship of the human race to God. Humans are religious beings, which means they are made by and for God, "to live in communion with God" (*Catechism of the Catholic Church*, 45). Within the human heart is a place that only God can fill. From the moment of conception, we were knitted in our "mother's womb" (Psalm 139:13) with a desire for truth and happiness that only God can satisfy.

Does this mean that anything and anyone less than God is worthless? Of course not. Anything good or anyone we love is a gift from God. God's gifts give us glimpses of him and help us to recognize his love for us. We must thank God for them. However, we must also realize that they will never satisfy us completely. Only God can satisfy the longings of the human heart.

All through the ages, the human race has recognized this longing and has attempted to fill it. From the earliest and most primitive tribes to the sophisticated musings of the Greeks and Romans, from the insights of Confucius to the religions of Hinduism and Islam, all civilizations have, in partial ways, tried to find their own pathways to God. These religions, even non-Christian ones, "attempt in different ways to overcome the restlessness of people's hearts by outlining a program of life covering doctrine, moral precepts and sacred rites" (*Declaration on the Relation of the Church to Non-Christian Religions [Nostra Aetate]*, 2).

Through Sacred Scripture and **Tradition**, we know that God himself has satisfied the human longing for communion with him in the Incarnation of Jesus Christ. In Jesus is fulfilled all the longings of the human race, articulated most precisely in the history of the Jewish people, which is the history of our salvation as well: "In times past, God spoke in partial and various ways to our ancestors through the prophets; in these last days, he spoke to us through a son (Hebrews 1:1–2)." That Son is Jesus Christ—our Way, our Truth, and our Life. The Church, which he founded, is our connection to him and to the way of life we are called to live as his followers.

Man's Search for Meaning

Viktor Frankl (1905–1997) was an Austrian psychotherapist and writer of the bestselling book *Man's Search for Meaning* (New York: Simon and Schuster, 1985). Frankl, who was Jewish, wrote about his experiences while a prisoner in a Nazi concentration camp during World War II and chronicled his search for a meaningful existence, even in the midst of cruelty and deprivation.

What were Frankl's secrets to survival in the midst of hopelessness? He discovered two. The first secret was love: "I grasped the meaning of the greatest secret that human poetry and human thought and belief have to impart: *The salvation of man is through love and in love.* I understood how a man who has nothing left in this world still may know bliss, be it only for a brief moment, in the contemplation of his beloved" (*Man's Search for Meaning,* pages 56–57). Frankl realized the second secret to survival as he observed other people in the concentration camp: "Spiritual life strengthened the prisoner, helped him adapt, and thereby improved his chances of survival" (123). He realized that the interior spiritual life was, for others as well as for himself, another key to endurance in the face of dire circumstances.

Released by American forces in 1945, Frankl discovered that his wife and parents had perished and that his only living relative was a sister who had escaped to Australia. He remarried and had one daughter. He continued his therapeutic work and was the recipient of several honorary doctorates from colleges and universities all over the world, including Catholic institutions.

What parallels can you see between Frankl's secrets to survival and the message of the Gospel?

The Universal Call to Holiness

Baptism, Confirmation, and the Eucharist—the Sacraments of Christian Initiation—are the foundation of the Christian life. Through these Sacraments we "live and move and have our being" (Acts of the Apostles 17:28) in Christ. As members of the Church, we are called to follow Jesus' path—the path of love without measure, the path of holiness: "Therefore, all in the church . . . are called to holiness. . . . This holiness of the church is shown constantly in the fruits of grace which the Spirit produces in the faithful and so it must be; it is expressed in many ways by the individuals who, each in their own state of life, tend to the perfection of charity, and are thus a source of edification for others" (*Dogmatic Constitution on the Church [Lumen Gentium]*, 39).

The "perfection of charity" is the perfection of love. Through love we edify, or build up, others. Each loving action of ours is a building block, contributing to the building up of the Body of Christ, making the Church more loving, more compassionate, filling it with more light, more goodness, more joy. This is our universal vocation, our universal call: a call from God to each and every member of the Church. And really, can anything less be expected of those who call themselves the followers of Christ?

The Meaning of Life

Your grandparents may have, through the teaching of the *Baltimore Catechism*, memorized the meaning of life when they were only seven or eight years old, and, if so, they probably still remember it! The *Baltimore Catechism* presented this wisdom in a question-and-answer format:

Q. Why did God make you?

A. God made me to know him, love him, and serve him in this life, and to be happy with him forever in the next.

Of course, to be fully understood, this answer requires some explanation. Once we come to know and love God, the source of all happiness, we will want to serve him—to do what he wants us to do in this life. And how do we serve him? Jesus gives us the answer: "Whatever you did for one of these least brothers of mine, you did for me" (Matthew 25:40). We serve God by serving one another.

The answer from the *Baltimore Catechism* might seem to imply that happiness is for the next world only and not for this one. Happiness with God in Heaven is the goal of life, but knowing, loving, and serving God helps us to taste happiness here and now.

You will not learn this from television commercials. You will not see this on billboards or scrolling across a computer screen. In these places, it seems that we are often given the message that satisfaction, or happiness, comes solely from the accumulation of money and material objects. But this is far from Jesus' message. Jesus taught that happiness comes from living the **Beatitudes** (see Matthew 5:1–12) and from our relationship with God and others. You may want to test this out by asking people you know who respond to God's call by loving and serving others—people who work in soup kitchens, who help out in the parish, who teach religion classes, who are kind to others. Why do they do it? They'll probably tell you it's because it makes them happy, because it brings them closer to God.

But the questions remain: How can *you* find the happiness that God wants you to have? How is God calling *you* to know, love, and serve him? The next article offers some guidance by examining the call of God in Scripture. ✝

Beatitudes
The teachings of Jesus during the Sermon on the Mount in which he describes the actions and attitudes that should characterize Christians and by which one can discover genuine meaning and happiness.

Catholic Wisdom

You Are the Light

When Pope Saint John Paul II (1920–2005) visited Saint Louis, Missouri, in January of 1999, he addressed a gathering of young people with these words: "You are ready for what Christ wants of you now. He wants you—all of you—to be the light of the world, as only young people can be light. It is time to let your light shine!" ("Address of John Paul II to the Young People at the Kiel Center," 4). These words can speak to you as you think about how you will serve God and others through the vocation to which God calls you.

Article 2 God's Call in the Old Testament

© mycola/Shutterstock.com

Each new day gives us another opportunity to listen to and respond to God's call in our life. What can you do to renew your commitment to follow God's will on a daily basis?

Spring, summer, fall, winter: There is a certain rhythm to life. One season follows another, yet no season, however many times we experience it, is exactly the same as the one that came before it. The seasons are familiar, yet always new.

Such is the call of God. It is familiar yet always new, calling us to new life, new possibilities, and new horizons. When we look to Scripture and study the accounts of people who have been called by God, we will find in them something familiar (for they are human, like us) yet also very new. Each time God calls, he reveals a new initiative, a new task, a new way to bring his people closer to him.

Let us consider a few of God's calls in the Old Testament. As we do, let us also ask: How has God called me in the past? How is he calling me now to prepare for the future?

The Call of Abraham

The Book of Deuteronomy contains a poignant description of Abraham (originally called Abram): "My father was a refugee Aramean" (Deuteronomy 26:5). Abraham, the father of the Jewish people and our father in faith, was a nomad who herded sheep, traveling from one part of the land to another. But Abraham's vocation, though it included sheepherding, was something greater. When God spoke, Abraham listened:

> The LORD said to Abram: "Go forth from your land, your relatives, and from your father's house to a land that I will show you. I will make of you a great nation, and I will bless you; I will make your name great, so that you will be a blessing. . . . All the families of the earth will find blessing in you." (Genesis 12:1–3)

Abraham's response was immediate: "Abram went as the LORD directed him. . . . Abram was seventy-five years old when he left Haran" (Genesis 12:4). The rhythm is established here: God calls, and we respond. This is what vocation is all about.

Have you ever been called to leave the land you knew to go to a new land? Some of you have, in real time and space. We are all, in some ways, constantly called to "a new land"—a new day, a new idea, a new way of looking at things, a new way of living. How is our call like Abraham's? We too are called to be a blessing for others.

The Call of David

Samuel had feared that Saul's kingship would not work out, and his fears proved well founded. God had allowed the people to have a king, but Saul had abused his privileges and disobeyed God's instructions. Another king had to be found, and Samuel set out for the city of Bethlehem, as the Lord commanded him.

There he found Jesse and his sons. One by one they came before Samuel, and Samuel, under God's instructions, rejected each one. As the Lord explained, "God does not see as a mortal, who sees the appearance. The LORD looks into the heart" (1 Samuel 16:7).

After seeing the sons, Samuel asked Jesse if these were all. Jesse replied that his youngest son was out tending the sheep. Samuel asked to see him. The account continues: "He was ruddy, a youth with beautiful eyes, and good looking. The LORD said: There—anoint him, for this is the one! Then Samuel, with the horn of oil in hand, anointed him in the midst of his brothers, and from that day on, the spirit of the LORD rushed upon David" (1 Samuel 16:12–13).

Sometimes it takes an objective outsider to help us to know our calling and to recognize our gifts. Never discount the people who believe in you and encourage you to follow your call.

The Call of Samuel

Abraham was called to a new life when he was quite old.
Samuel, who was a servant in the Temple to the priest Eli,
was called at a young age. The writer of the First Book of
Samuel prepares us for God's call by noting that "during the
time young Samuel was minister to the LORD under Eli,
the Word of the LORD was scarce and vision infrequent"
(3:1). We are to realize that the events to come will be highly
unusual. Samuel was sleeping and then heard someone call
him. Thinking it was Eli, he ran to the priest and said, "'Here
I am. You called me.' 'I did not call you,' Eli answered. 'Go
back to sleep'" (3:5). Then the same thing happened again!
And then for a third time! Finally, Eli realized that it was the
Lord who was calling Samuel, and so he instructed Samuel
to say, "Speak, LORD, for your servant is listening" (3:9).
Samuel went back to sleep, and when he heard the voice calling, he spoke the words as Eli instructed him and received a
message from God. When he got up the next day, he shared
that message with Eli. Samuel went on to be an acknowledged prophet of God, continually listening and responding
to God's call.

Who are the people in your life that remind you to listen
to God's call? And how can you be a reminder to others of
the need to say, "Speak, Lord, for your servant is listening"?

The Call of Jeremiah

Sometimes we find that the chosen ones of God register a
protest at God's choice. "Why me?" might be their theme.
One of these was the Prophet Jeremiah. The Book of Jeremiah is written from the prophet's own perspective, and it
begins in this way:

> The word of the LORD came to me:
> Before I formed you in the womb I knew you,
>> before you were born I dedicated you,
>> a prophet to the nations I appointed you.
>>> (1:4–5)

But Jeremiah protests:

> "Ah, Lord GOD!" I said,
>> "I do not know how to speak. I am too young!"
> But the LORD answered me,

Do not say, "I am too young."
> To whomever I send you, you shall go;
> whatever I command you, you shall speak.

Do not be afraid of them,
> for I am with you to deliver you—oracle of the LORD.

(1:6–8)

How are you like Jeremiah? Do you tend toward self-doubt? Do you feel unprepared for the future God has in store for you? The call of Jeremiah assures us that, no matter what our limitations, God will be with us to prepare us and to help us to answer his call. ♱

Article 3   God's Call in the New Testament

The Old Testament gives us accounts of God's call to various people and his saving work among many generations of ancient Israelites. It shows his covenant relationship with them. The New Testament announces the fulfillment of God's Covenant with Israel, Jesus Christ, the Eternal Son, sent by the Father to redeem us in the Holy Spirit. Jesus is the fullness of God's Revelation and the one in whom God established his covenant forever. Jesus came to bring salvation to all people. All of his life teaches us about God's saving plan and helps us to understand God's call to humanity.

Let us now explore some accounts of God's calling in the New Testament, beginning with a young woman who was called and who responded in faith. This young woman lived in a small town of Galilee called Nazareth. Her name was Mary.

The Call of Mary

When she was a young woman, a virgin, Mary was engaged to a local carpenter named Joseph. Gabriel,

This fifteenth-century image of the Annunciation shows Mary's encounter with the angel Gabriel. What can you learn from Mary's response to Gabriel's message that can be helpful as you continue to discover God's call in your own life?

© Bettmann/CORBIS

God's messenger, was sent to her with a very important message: "Do not be afraid, Mary, for you have found favor with God. Behold, you will conceive in your womb and bear a son, and you shall name him Jesus" (Luke 1:30–31).

The angel explains to Mary that she will conceive a son through the power of the Holy Spirit: "Therefore the child to be born will be called holy, the Son of God. . . . for nothing will be impossible for God" (Luke 1:35,37). And Mary's reply has rung like a clear crystal bell down through the ages: "Behold, I am the handmaid of the Lord. May it be done to me according to your word" (Luke 1:38).

The human race stands in awe of this woman who cooperated with God in changing the course of history. After questioning the angel and hearing his response, Mary said yes to God's call to be the Mother of God.

Your questions too need not interfere with God's call. If you are faithful and trusting, asking questions and listening intently for answers can move you forward into a greater understanding of what God is asking of you and can lead you to answer yes, as Mary did.

Pray It!

Prayer to Our Lady of the Way

Life is a journey, and certainly Mary, the Mother of God, understands this journey. She who "kept all these things in her heart" (Luke 2:51) surely pondered God's will throughout her own journey and can help us to do the same.

In Rome, the Church of the Gesu (the "home church" of the Jesuits) was built over a previous church dedicated to Our Lady under the title Madonna della Strada, meaning "Our Lady of the Way" or "Our Lady of the Road." The Jesuits adopted Our Lady of the Way as their patron. This is the traditional prayer to Our Lady of the Way:

Sweet Mary, our heavenly Mother,

guide our steps on the often wild and rugged ways of life,

and when life arrives at its end,

be for us the door of heaven

and show us the fruit of your womb, Jesus.

Amen.

You may want to pray, "Our Lady of the Way, pray for me and guide me."

The Call of Nathanael

Nathanael's friend Philip introduced him to Jesus. As the Gospel of John relates, "Philip found Nathanael and told him, 'We have found the one about whom Moses wrote in the law, and also the prophets, Jesus son of Joseph, from Nazareth'" (John 1:45).

Nathanael was not immediately convinced. He had heard things about Nazareth, and apparently not all of them favorable. "But Nathanael said to him, 'Can anything good come from Nazareth?'" (John 1:46). Philip was persistent: "Come and see" (John 1:47).

When Jesus saw Nathanael coming, he said: "Here is a true Israelite. There is no duplicity in him" (John 1:47). Nathanael then challenges Jesus and asks, "How do you know me?" (1:48). Jesus tells Nathanael that, even before Philip found him, he had seen him under a fig tree. Immediately Nathanael becomes a believer: "Rabbi, you are the Son of God; you are the King of Israel" (1:49). Jesus replies: "Do you believe because I told you that I saw you under the fig tree? You will see greater things than this" (1:50). Jesus then tells of the future triumph of the Kingdom of God: "Amen, amen, I say to you, you will see the sky opened and the angels of God ascending and descending on the Son of Man" (1:51).

Jesus knows us and loves us. He finds us where we are and calls us to where he wants us to be. He often calls us from small things to great, little by little, until we realize that, in continuing to follow his call, we are contributing to something amazing. This is hard to see at the beginning. Maybe Nathanael was just thrilled that Jesus noticed him! But Jesus had greater plans than Nathanael could imagine, and these began to take form when Nathanael decided to follow Jesus.

The Call of Peter

The first call of Peter was simple and straightforward. John the Baptist pointed out Jesus to Andrew, and Andrew brought his brother Peter along, saying, "We have found the Messiah" (John 1:41).

The second call was anything but simple. It was complicated. Maybe you recall the scene in which Jesus cooked breakfast on the beach after his Resurrection and all the disciples gathered around. You may also remember that Peter, as Jesus had predicted, betrayed the Lord in the courtyard of the high priest. Three times Peter denied even knowing Jesus. But then Jesus appeared to all of them after his Resurrection and shared his peace and forgiveness with them—Peter included. But Jesus had something else in store for Peter.

The Call of Mary Magdalene

Mary Magdalene was among the women from Galilee who accompanied Jesus and the Apostles in their traveling and preaching, providing financial support for them. In all four Gospels, she is among the first of the faithful witnesses of the Resurrected Lord Jesus, who entrusts her with the mission of proclaiming the Good News to the other disciples.

Early on Sunday morning, Mary Magdalene visits the tomb where Jesus was buried and sees that the stone has been removed. She immediately runs to Peter and the other "beloved disciple" and says, "They have taken the Lord from the tomb, and we don't know where they put him" (John 20:2). Peter and the other disciple look, find the tomb empty, and return home. But Mary cannot bear to leave. She stays outside the tomb, weeping. Then she turns and sees what she thought was the gardener. The "gardener" (who was really Jesus) says one word to her: "Mary!" She says one word to him: *"Rabbouni!"* (Teacher). Jesus gives her instructions: "'Go to my brothers and tell them,

'I am going to my Father and your Father, to my God and your God'" (20:17). Mary Magdalene does just that. She announces to the disciples, "I have seen the Lord" (20:18). And so to the early Church Mary Magdalene was known as the Apostle to the Apostles.

Under the law at the time, women were not allowed to be witnesses in any legal proceeding. Their word, no matter how true, was not considered valid. Yet here Jesus calls Mary Magdalene to be a witness to his Resurrection! Surely this is another instance of what the angel told the first woman disciple of Jesus, Mary of Nazareth: "Nothing will be impossible for God" (Luke 1:37).

The dialogue between Jesus and Peter is symbolic. Jesus asks Peter three times, "Do you love me?" Peter answers three times, "Yes, Lord, you know that I love you." And each time Peter answers, Jesus calls him to care, concern, and responsibility: "Feed my sheep. . . . Tend my sheep. . . . Feed my sheep." And finally Jesus invites him again: "Follow me" (John 21: 15–19).

The lambs and the sheep are the People of God, the Church. And for Peter, following Jesus will mean care, concern, and responsibility for all the people to whom he and the other Apostles will bring the Good News.

We, like Peter, are challenged to move beyond the often easier response that comes in the form of words. It is far easier to claim our love than to demonstrate it day in and day out. How are we living out our love for Jesus in the words and actions of our lives? ✝

Article 4 The Foundation of the Christian Life

All human beings are called. They are called to know, to love, and to serve God by virtue of the fact that they are human. By faith and by Baptism, we enter into the great family of God's Church, bonded together by our unity in Christ. And Baptism, along with the other Sacraments of Christian Initiation, lays the foundation for every Christian's life. Together, and with the help of God's grace, all the members of the Church commit to striving to live according to God's will.

© Bill Wittman/www.wpwittman.com

In Baptism we are called from darkness into light. How can you be light for the world?

Baptism

Baptism gives us the grace we need to be able to say yes to whatever call we may hear at any future point in our lives. We could hardly be faithful single people, spouses, parents, consecrated people, or priests if we were not faithful Christians first. It is impossible to show the love of Christ to others if we are not first seeking to follow him as fully as we can.

For those of us who were baptized as infants, our parents and godparents made our baptismal promises for us, accepting the call to discipleship in Christ on our behalf. But this does not make our baptismal call any less important. No matter the circumstances of our Baptism, God personally calls each and every one of us to discipleship and to membership in Christ's Body, the Church. Even if the first yes to Baptism was said by someone other than ourselves, we can still say yes in a real way through our daily striving to live in closer conformity to God's will by answering his call in our lives.

What Happens at Baptism?

During the Rite of Baptism, the candidate is immersed in water three times (or water is poured over the candidate's head three times) while a priest or deacon prays: "I baptize you in the name of the Father, and of the Son, and of the Holy Spirit" (*Rite of Baptism*, 60). The action of being immersed in water and then arising out of the water calls

Live It!

Celebrate Your Baptism!

Through Baptism, God has made you a new creation as his adopted son or daughter and a member of Christ and has called you to participate in the mission of the Church. Do you know the date of your Baptism? Do you have a copy of your baptismal certificate?

One high school religion teacher, a married woman with children, keeps photos and mementos under the glass top of her desk at school. In the middle of the array she has placed her baptismal certificate. "That's what started everything," she says. "That is at the center of it all."

Reflect on ways to honor your Baptism and baptismal day. Write to the parish of your Baptism and ask for a copy of your baptismal certificate. Hang it in your room. If your family has kept your baptismal candle, you may want to light it on your baptismal day and pray the Lord's Prayer.

to mind Jesus' death, burial, and Resurrection and our own participation in Christ's **Paschal Mystery**.

In Baptism we die to sin and are reborn to a new life of grace. Baptism cleanses us from the stain of Original Sin and, for those receiving the Sacrament after the **age of reason**, frees us from any personal sins we may have committed prior to Baptism. As a result of this baptismal state of grace, we begin to have God's own life dwelling within us, and we become temples of the Holy Spirit.

Baptism also unites us with Christ in a special way and incorporates us into his Church. By this sacramental encounter with Christ, we are introduced to the intimacy of the inner life of God in the mystery of the Trinity, and we become the adoptive sons and daughters of God.

After the immersion in water, we are anointed with the **Sacred Chrism**. By this we are made sharers in Jesus Christ's identity as the Anointed One, and we are called to participate in his priestly, prophetic, and kingly offices.

Confirmation and the Eucharist

In addition to Baptism, we celebrate two other Sacraments of Christian Initiation: Confirmation and the Eucharist. Confirmation strengthens us in our faith and deepens the grace we received at Baptism. We are anointed with Sacred Chrism and receive the seal of the Gift of the Holy Spirit, which marks us as sharing more completely in the mission of Christ.

Although young Catholics often receive First Holy Communion prior to Confirmation, the Eucharist is the culmination of the Sacraments of Christian Initiation. In the Eucharist we consume Jesus' Body and Blood under the appearance of bread and wine. By doing so we take Christ into ourselves. Participation in the Eucharist deepens our baptismal call to communion with God, as the Eucharist leads us into a radical, profound union with Christ.

The Sacraments of Christian Initiation call us to holiness, but they also enable us to accept other calls God may have for us in the future. Baptism, Confirmation, and the Eucharist draw us into a close identification with Jesus Christ, which helps us to hear God's voice. Furthermore, the grace we receive from the Sacraments is the foundation upon which our Christian lives and vocations are based. ✝

Paschal Mystery
The work of salvation accomplished by Jesus Christ mainly through his Passion, death, Resurrection, and Ascension.

age of reason
The age at which a person can be morally responsible. This is generally regarded to be the age of seven.

Sacred Chrism
Perfumed olive oil that has been consecrated. It is used for anointing in the Sacraments of Baptism, Confirmation, and Holy Orders.

How God Makes Us Holy

Grace, especially the grace given to us in the Sacraments, is God's way of making us holy. Grace is the gift of God's loving presence with us, which empowers us to respond to his call and to live always as his children. Grace is never earned; although none of us truly deserves grace, God freely chooses to bless us with this gift. We could never become holy by our own power. God, who is all-holy and all-good, shares that holiness and goodness with us through various kinds of grace:

- **Sanctifying grace** is the grace that heals our human nature wounded by sin and restores us to friendship with God by giving us a share in the divine life of the Trinity. It is a supernatural gift of God, infused into our souls by the Holy Spirit, that continues the work of making us holy.

- **Actual grace** is God's interventions and support for us in the everyday moments of our lives. Actual graces are important for conversion and for continuing growth in holiness.

- **Sacramental graces** are graces specific to each of the Seven Sacraments.

- **Charisms** are special graces of the Holy Spirit, given to individuals or communities, that help us to live out our commitment to a state in life and to carry out the responsibilities of that state. They help to build up the Body of Christ. *Charism* comes from a Greek word meaning "favor" or "gratuitous gift."

© Pascal Deloche/Godong/Corbis

Part Review

1. How is a vocation both a call from God and a response to God?

2. What does the *universal call to holiness* mean and what does it ask of us?

3. Why did God make you, and how can you serve him?

4. Name two significant people called by God in the Old Testament and describe the call of one of these in detail.

5. Name two significant people called by God in the New Testament and describe the call of one of these in detail.

6. Give an example of the way Baptism calls us to live our lives as followers of Christ.

7. What does the Holy Spirit, through the Sacrament of Confirmation, help us to do?

Part 2

We Respond to God's Call

You may be familiar with the saying in the sports world, "There is no *I* in *TEAM*." This statement is intended to motivate team members to play not just for themselves but for the entire team. Though each of us has a distinct call from God, rooted in our baptismal call, and though each of us will make a personal decision concerning that call, we can note here that there is no *I* in *CHURCH* or *PEOPLE OF GOD*.

Whatever our call, we are bound together as disciples of Jesus Christ. Each and every member of the Church, from the Pope to the newest baptized baby, needs all the others to fulfill God's call. We are not called merely to live good lives and bring ourselves to Heaven; we are called to bring everyone else, the entire Church and, yes, the entire world, with us.

As the Church, and as the new People of God, we are united in Christ by the grace of the Sacraments of Baptism, Confirmation, and the Eucharist. As we follow Jesus as disciples, let us remember that we do not follow him alone.

The articles in this part address the following topics:

5 We Listen to Our Teacher

We live in a culture that uses the word *love* for many different things, from the trivial to the profound. As Christians, and as followers of Jesus, we must identify love with charity, or *agape* (AH-gah-pay). The word *agape*, or unconditional love, is a Greek word used in Scripture and by the early Christians to describe both God's love and the kind of love Christians aim to share with one another.

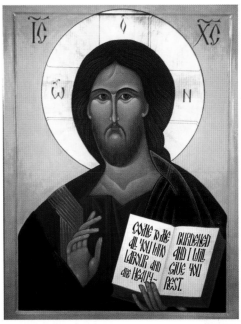

© Bill Wittman/www.wpwittman.com

True love involves self-giving. It is a serving love. It is a caring love that puts aside one's own immediate interest for the interest of another. It sets aside "my agenda" for yours. It goes around the block or around the world to love and to serve God and his people.

But how do we learn about the love God calls us to? How did the Apostles come to know and share God's love? They learned about it from Jesus, the only Son of God. And we can too.

Part of our vocation as Christians is to share God's love with others. Jesus taught us how to love by his words and actions. Which accounts from Scripture can you recall that teach about our call to love?

Teacher of Love

By word and by example, Jesus taught us how to love. He was not the kind of teacher who said, "You do this, and I'll watch." He was the kind of teacher who did it first and then invited us to do the same. His self-sacrifice on the Cross was the greatest witness of God's love for us and of how we should love God and one another. Let us look at the Gospels to find other examples of Jesus' teaching about love.

The Gospel of John

In the Gospel of John, we find the new teaching of Jesus, the commandment to love: "I give you a new commandment: love one another. As I have loved you, so you also should love one another. This is how all will know that you are my disciples, if you have love for one another" (John 13:34–35).

Love and the Paschal Mystery

As an old saying has it, "The path of true love never runs smooth." This reminds us that often love involves some kind of suffering. Jesus himself showed us the greatest example of God's love for us in his sacrifice on the Cross. Through his suffering and death, Jesus taught the truth in love. That truth was rejected, and he paid with his life. This was not the end of his life, of course. Though he was raised from the dead and ascended to Heaven, he was not spared the painful consequences of his loving choices, and neither are we.

Because we live in Christ, we too are part of the Paschal Mystery. We accept suffering and sacrifice as inevitable parts of life and as necessary consequences that come with following Christ. But there is good news. The Gospel proclaims that suffering and death are not our ultimate end. They are only steps on our path toward Heaven and eternal life.

The Christian life calls for choices that promote truth, goodness, and justice, and sometimes those choices have consequences that cause us suffering or require sacrifice. Through the Eucharist our sacrifices, suffering, and entire lives are united to Christ's. Through this union we participate in God's saving work. Pope Saint John Paul II reminds us that this is part of what it means to live a Christian life rooted in Gospel values: "But—I ask you—is it better to be resigned to a life without ideals . . . or rather, . . . to seek the truth, goodness, justice, working for a world that reflects the beauty of God, even at the cost of facing the trials it may involve?" ("Message of the Holy Father to the Youth of the World on the Occasion of the XII World Youth Day," 3). How would you answer?

We can love one another, not of our own power, but because God loved us first (see *Catechism of the Catholic Church* [CCC], 1823.)

One example of the love of Jesus is unique to the Gospel of John: the account of the washing of the feet at the Last Supper. Here Jesus instructs his disciples (and us as well): "You call me 'teacher' and 'master,' and rightly so, for indeed I am. If I, therefore, the master and teacher, have washed your feet, you ought to wash one another's feet. I have given you a model to follow" (John 13:13–15). This model is a model of loving service, even of the lowliest kind.

The Gospel of Mark

In the Gospel of Mark, the first Gospel to be written, we find Jesus' teaching on the Great Commandment. (It is also found in the Gospels of Matthew and Luke.) When a scribe asks him which commandment is the greatest, Jesus replies with the Shema, the traditional prayer of the Jews: "Hear, O Israel! The Lord our God is Lord alone! You shall love the Lord your God with all your heart, with all your soul, with all your mind, and with all your strength" (Mark 12:29–30). But surprisingly, Jesus also added this: "'You shall love your neighbor as yourself.' There is no other commandment greater than these" (Mark 12:31). Both of these commandments are found in the Old Testament, the first at Deuteronomy 6:4–5, and the second at Leviticus 19:18. The passage from Deuteronomy was well known to all Jews, but the Second Commandment was very obscure. When Jesus elevated it to the same status as the passage from Deuteronomy, he was presenting a new teaching and a new standard for love.

The Gospel of Matthew

In the Gospel of Matthew, we find the Sermon on the Mount, the great summary of Jesus' teachings on every aspect of life. In the previous part, we spoke of "the perfection of charity" or perfect love. In the Gospel of Matthew, we find a description of that love in Jesus' teaching on love of enemies. In Matthew 5:44–48, Jesus teaches:

> Love your enemies, and pray for those who persecute you.
> . . . For if you love those who love you, what recompense will you have? Do not the tax collectors do the same? And if you greet your brothers only, what is unusual about that? Do not the pagans do the same? So be perfect, just as your heavenly Father is perfect.

What a tall order this is! What great love Jesus is asking of his disciples! Here Jesus is asking us to love as God loves: unconditionally. This is how perfection is measured in Jesus' eyes. How close can we come?

The Gospel of Luke

The Gospel of Luke is well known for its collection of parables, and one of the most famous and well loved is that of the Good Samaritan. This parable, in Luke 10:29–37, tells of "love of enemies" in story form. The parable answers the question, "Who is my neighbor?" and the answer is found at the end: My neighbor is anyone in need of mercy, and I can be a neighbor only if I am merciful to others, including those whom I identify as "enemy" or "in the wrong group" or "not like me."

Some early Christian writings identify the Good Samaritan with Jesus, who comes across the human race wounded and lying half-dead. Jesus then cares for us and heals us, to limitless expense, even at the expense of his own suffering and death. Jesus is the perfect neighbor, the one who always treats us with mercy. ✝

Live It!

Living Love

Love is not something we should save for special occasions. Love is something we can do every day. Try this. Designate a special jar or container, perhaps an empty coffee can. Decorate it if you like. Then, on small slips of paper, write as many loving actions as you can think of. Here are a few examples:

Smile.

When asked for help, say yes.

Help out at home.

"Bite your tongue" when tempted to say something mean.

Offer to help someone with homework.

Fill the container with ideas of loving actions you know you can do. Every day pull out one of your ideas and put it into practice. (Of course, God may have other good actions in store for you as well. Do those too!) Add more ideas as you can. You may find, as others have before you, that your life will have more meaning and more joy.

Article 6 We Respond in Discipleship

But how can we, as individuals, with all our strengths and weaknesses, truly keep the Great Commandment, to love God with all of our heart, soul, and strength and to love our neighbor as ourselves? The challenge of living as a disciple of Christ might seem like trying to climb a large, steep mountain.

The word *disciple* comes from a Greek word meaning "learner." A disciple of Jesus is one who has made the decision to learn from him. In our everyday lives, lots of people (real and virtual) tell us what to do, and these people come at us from every direction—in ads on TV and on the Internet, in music and songs, in texts, and through social media. If you have made the decision to be a disciple of Jesus, you can see through all these other messages, taking only what is good and true from them. "Learn from me," Jesus says, "for I am meek and humble of heart; and you will find rest for yourselves" (Matthew 11:29).

© Ocean/Corbis

Respect and Love for Self

As disciples of Jesus, we need to have a healthy respect and love for ourselves. How can we love others if we do not love ourselves? Always remember that you are created in the image and likeness of God. God sees goodness and creativity in you. You may not see this all the time, but it is there. Others may not see it, but it is there. In making you, God gave a new gift to the world. You will not be able to give this gift to others, in any vocation, if you do not respect and love the gift of yourself that God made. But love for self does not mean indulging in selfish tendencies. It means taking care of ourselves in body, mind, heart, and soul.

It is important that we surround ourselves with people who support us in our discipleship. How do your friends encourage you as a follower of Christ?

Called to Be and to Make Disciples

When Jesus gathered followers to help him to proclaim and bring about the Kingdom, he did not call the most talented and powerful; rather, he chose ordinary fishermen (see Mark 1:16–20) and even a tax collector (see 2:13–17)—a person despised by most Israelites. God's call comes to everyone, even (or perhaps especially) to those who think they may not be worthy.

Jesus sent out these disciples to preach the Kingdom and to "make disciples of all nations" (Matthew 28:19), calling all people to join the Church. This group of followers, his first disciples, became the Church, Jesus' true family, and the seed and beginning of the Kingdom on earth. The Church is thus a sign, as well as the actual beginning, of that perfect peace and happiness that all of us desire: the Kingdom of God, mysteriously present in the world, which will be fully realized at the end of time.

All baptized believers are disciples and participate in the Church's mission of calling others to become disciples of Christ. Think about how believers have been witnesses of the Gospel over the centuries. Think about what it means to be part of the Church, which is one, holy, catholic, and apostolic. Think about the gifts you have to offer the Church. Pray about what it means to be part of the Church. Then go and be a disciple and an example and witness of faith to others.

Relationships with Others

Respect and love for self is important, because this is how we learn to respect and love others as well. We recognize the God-given dignity of all people and realize that everyone needs and deserves love and respect. This is the basis on which all relationships are built.

Whatever our individual vocation is, we live it out in relationship with others. And whatever our vocation, we are called to develop relationships with others that reflect the communion of the three Persons of the Trinity. No vocation, not even the vocation of a hermit in the deepest forest, is lived in isolation. We live in the midst of society, and we are called to transform our society by living our own particular vocation to the best of our ability. We answer God's call together with millions of others who are also called to enter the Kingdom. As disciples of Jesus, we are all called to the gift of self in love, and it is only through this gift that we find our true selves in God.

In human relationships we find the best and sometimes the worst of ourselves. We also find the best and sometimes the worst in others. What will our response be? Of course, gratitude and joy for the best, and, hopefully, forgiveness and understanding for the worst. But these responses take practice. Practice gratitude, joy, forgiveness, and understanding in little ways, and then, when something greater is asked of you, you will be able to meet the challenge. ✝

Catholic Wisdom

Take the Elevator!

At the time of Saint Thérèse of Lisieux (1873–1897), the elevator was a new invention: "I wanted to find an elevator which would raise me to Jesus, for I am too small to climb the rough stairway of perfection. . . . The elevator which must raise me to heaven is Your arms, O Jesus! . . . I had to remain *little* and become this more and more" (*Story of a Soul*, pages 207 and 208). Thérèse realized that Jesus accepted her efforts, loved her as she was, and would raise her himself.

Article 7 We Respond as the People of God

Do names matter? The great playwright William Shakespeare raises this issue as he sets the scene for a famous tragedy. In *Romeo and Juliet*, Juliet asks: "What's in a name? That which we call a rose by any other name would smell as sweet." Juliet is arguing that names have no meaning: she loves Romeo, the person, and it should not matter that he is a Montague and belongs to a family currently at war with her family, the Capulets. In response Romeo renounces the name of Montague—but of course this does not prevent the tragedy from moving forward. Names are not so easily shed.

What about the name *Church*? What does that name mean? Can we call it something else and still be talking about the same thing? It turns out that we can. We can because the Church is defined by three inseparable meanings: the entire community of believers God gathers throughout the world, the local church (the diocese), and the assembly of believers gathered for the liturgy.

But let's go back to biblical times, to the use of the word *church* in the New Testament. The New Testament Greek word we translate as *church* is *ekklesia*. This word is related to the Greek verb *ek-ka-lein*, which means "to call out," as to call together an assembly or convocation. This is what we fundamentally mean by *church*: the people God calls together from the ends of the earth to be in relationship with him. But we can call the Church by another name: the People of God. This name is scriptural in origin and stretches back to God's plan from the beginning of time to

The Pope is the visible head of the Catholic Church and is responsible for ministering to Catholics throughout the world. We look to him in a unique way for guidance and inspiration on our common journey as disciples of Christ.

© ALBERTO PIZZOLI/ALBERTO PIZZOLI/AFP/Getty Images

call a people to himself. The People of God in the Old Testament were the Jews, and they still are today, for God never revokes his call. The universal Church is the new People of God, entered into by faith and Baptism, so that, in union with Christ, all people "may form one family and one People of God (*Ad Gentes*, 1)" (*CCC*, 804).

What does this mean for each individual vocation, or call, within this new People of God? It means that we are all in it together. We all support one another as we strive to live

We Are the Body of Christ

The Church's sacramental life unites us to Christ and provides us with the guidance and Gifts of the Holy Spirit. As the Body of Christ, which is another image for the Church, we, the members of the Church, give strength, hope, and support to one another in our common goal of becoming holy people. The Church provides us with opportunities for education, prayer, community, and service to the world. Christ has given the Church the gift of holiness. As members of the Church, we share in that gift, though we are sinners.

Answer God's call to grow in holiness. Take time away from the rush and noise of the world to meet Jesus in the silence of your heart. Then go out into the world and let Christ's holiness shine through you to bring his love to others. God offers you his forgiveness; let his gift touch the hearts of others through you. Let your moral living influence others to make the right choices. Let acts of humble and loving service show others they are not alone; they are loved by God.

out our personal call from God and contribute to the mission of the Church. We are not just individuals, living our individual lives. We hold one another up in prayer and in action. We are the people God has called together, a worldwide assembly—the One, Holy, Catholic, and Apostolic Church!

We Respond in the Church

Within the Church there are four recognized states of life: committed single life, married life, ordained life (as a bishop, priest, or deacon), and consecrated life. Each of these states of life is rooted in the baptismal call to live as a son or daughter of the Father, in Christ, with the help of the Holy Spirit. These states of life are the focus of this book.

Committed single life is one way to live out the baptismal call. It is a state of life that is not bound by public vows, but it is a recognized way that people may respond to God's call to serve others and the Church.

Married life is also based on the baptismal call to live in holiness. However, the Sacrament of Matrimony bestows the particular sacramental graces proper to Marriage, in order to help the married man and woman live out their vocation.

Pray It!

Pray the Lord's Prayer

Saint Thomas Aquinas called the Lord's Prayer "the most perfect prayer." The Catechism calls it "the quintessential prayer of the Church" (2776). If we pray it sincerely, we may see why.

We pray to *Our* Father. We are not alone. We are all the Father's children.

"Hallowed be thy name." *Hallowed* means "holy." Do we treat the name of God as holy, holding it in reverence? Or do we throw it around heedlessly?

"Thy kingdom come, thy will be done on earth as it is in heaven." What is my call? How can I do God's will on earth? Help me to know, Father.

"Give us this day our daily bread." It is not my bread, but *our* bread. Help me to share with others in need.

"And forgive us our trespasses, as we forgive . . ." Forgive me, Father, and help me to forgive as you do.

"And lead us not into temptation, but deliver us from evil." Saying no now will lead to a better future later. Help me to remember, Father.

"Amen."

The challenge of Marriage is to help one's spouse and children to become holy as well—that is, to help them to live the life of love that God intends for all of us to live.

Ordained life is another way one lives out the baptismal call. The ordination of bishops, priests, and deacons is essential to the organic structure and the good of the Church; without them we cannot speak of the Church. In addition, the Sacrament of Holy Orders bestows the particular sacramental graces proper to the ordained ministry, so that the deacon, priest, or bishop can fulfill his duties to all the People of God. No one has a right to ordination; it is a call from God. The desire for ordination must be submitted to the Church. In turn the Church will call a man to receive orders. The Sacrament of Holy Orders, like all the other Sacraments, is an unmerited gift.

Consecrated life also stems directly from the Sacrament of Baptism and its call to live in holiness. Although the taking of religious vows is not a Sacrament, the vows signify an intention to follow Christ more closely in a life totally dedicated to God. Religious vows help the Christian to pursue a life of perfect love in service to the Kingdom and witness the coming of the Kingdom both now and in the world to come.

All states of life enjoy an equal dignity within the Church. No one state is more important or more holy than another. Holiness does not depend on one particular state of life but on our relationship with God and the way we fulfill the call of our own state of life.

By fully embracing and living out our own personal vocation in whatever state of life we are called to, we contribute to the Church's mission, its vocation, of spreading the Good News of Christ. With the guidance of the Holy Spirit, the Body of Christ relies on the diversity of vocations within to continue to build the Church and to prepare for the coming of the Kingdom of God. ✟

Part Review

1. What does *agape* mean? Describe its characteristics.

2. Give an example of Jesus' teaching on love from each of the four Gospels.

3. What does the word *disciple* mean, and how can we be disciples of Jesus in our everyday lives?

4. Why is a properly understood "love for self" important in any vocation?

5. Why is relationship with others important in every state of life?

6. Why is "the People of God" a good description, or name, for the Church?

Part 3

The Call of the Laity

The Church is mostly composed of the lay faithful, also called the laity. Laypeople can be either married or single. The laity are people who are not ordained or in a consecrated state of life. Some might think that the role of the laity is less important to the Church than these other vocations, but that is not the case at all! The laity are the people whose primary vocation is to make Christ present in every walk of human life. The laity help to make Christ known everywhere they go, including schools, hospitals, factories, offices, and most especially among their own friends and family.

Through Baptism laypeople are called to share in the priestly, prophetic, and kingly office of Christ. This means that they are called to holiness and a life centered in prayer and the Sacraments; they are called to proclaim Christ to others through their words and deeds; and they are called to exercise leadership in the Church when appropriate and to serve others, particularly those who are poor and suffering.

The lay life is an important vocation to consider, as it is through the faith, prayers, and good works of the laity that the Gospel can be spread most completely to every corner of the world. This section of your book ends with a specific look at the single life as one way laypeople live out their Christian vocation.

The articles in this part address the following topics:

Article 8 Who Are the Lay Faithful?

laity (the lay faithful, laypeople)
All members of the Church with the exception of those who are ordained as bishops, priests, or deacons. The laity share in Christ's role as priest, prophet, and king, witnessing to God's love and power in the world.

As a young person, you are part of the laity and are called to share the Good News with others. In what ways, big or small, are you a witness to God's love to your friends, classmates, family members, and people in your community?

In a technical sense, the **laity** (also referred to as the lay faithful or laypeople) are baptized Catholics who have not received the Sacrament of Holy Orders. Even women religious and nonordained religious brothers are considered laypeople in this strict sense of the term. But in general, when you hear a reference to the laity, it is most likely a reference to those Catholics who are not ordained clergy and who also have not entered into a state of consecrated life formally recognized by the Church.

It is important to avoid defining the laity by who they are not (i.e., not ordained or not in consecrated life); rather, we should consider them for who they are—namely, full members of the Church who share their own specific role in spreading the Good News. Laypeople may be married or single, and only laypeople can enter into the Sacrament of Matrimony (this vocation is the focus of the next section). Because of this, marriage and family life are, for the most part, vocations unique to the lay faithful.

In terms of numbers, laypeople make up the vast majority of Catholics, and they live the Church's mission in their everyday lives as they interact with secular society. Through this interaction laypeople are called to become the "salt of the earth" and "the light of the world" (see Matthew 5:13–14) with their very presence as Christians, bringing the message of Good News to the world.

© Bill Wittman/www.wpwittman.com

In the World, but Not of the World

Laypeople are called to be *in* the world but not *of* the world. This might sound like nothing more than a tricky play on words, but it is actually the core of the vocation of the laity.

Laypeople are called to be *in* the world in the sense that it is their vocation to participate fully in the goodness of ordinary daily life. The laity are not called to live secluded lives like monks in monasteries, nor are they usually called to devote the majority of their time to the direct service of the Church in the same way priests and consecrated persons are.

The life of a lay Christian can involve interaction with the media, the marketplace, the local and national governments, and secular cultural establishments. The laity are fully engaged in the world, because their lives are engaged in every legitimate aspect of the human experience, not just those that are explicitly Church-related.

On the other hand, Christian laypeople are called to be not *of* the world, meaning that they are not meant to regard themselves simply as citizens of secular society. They should understand their lives in relation to their identity as adopted sons and daughters of God and in light of the truth as it is revealed by God and taught by the Church. Lay Christians understand that the most important things are not material

Pray It!

The Letter to Diognetus

This ancient letter is read every year during the Easter season as a part of the Liturgy of the Hours, the official public, daily prayer of the Catholic Church.

> Christians are indistinguishable from other men either by nationality, language or customs. They do not inhabit separate cities of their own, or speak a strange dialect, or follow some outlandish way of life. . . . And yet there is something extraordinary about their lives. . . . They live in the flesh, but they are not governed by the desires of the flesh. They pass their days upon earth, but they are citizens of heaven. . . . As the soul is present in every part of the body, while remaining distinct from it, so Christians are found in all the cities of the world, but cannot be identified with the world. (*From a Letter to Diognetus*)

What might be some of the struggles with being *in* the world but not *of* the world? How could you bring these struggles to God in prayer?

but spiritual. Whereas "worldly" persons might have as their top priorities the accumulation of wealth, the attainment of bodily beauty, or the exclusive pursuit of pleasurable experiences, the highest priorities for lay Christians are love, honor, and service of God and neighbor.

Lay Ecclesial Ministry

The most appropriate **apostolate** for the laity is their work and Christian witness in the world in the sense that this is the most distinctive element of their vocation. However, at times individual laypeople can be called upon to serve the Church in a more direct manner. When this occurs the layperson is participating in what is called lay ecclesial ministry.

In the parish lay ecclesial ministry can be encompassed in such roles as parish catechetical leader, youth minister, school principal, and director of liturgy or music. In the larger structure of the Church, lay ecclesial ministry might also include a variety of leadership roles in a diocesan office. In a 2005 document on lay ecclesial ministry titled *Co-Workers in the Vineyard of the Lord*, the U.S. bishops note that lay ecclesial ministry is identified by four characteristics: authorization (from the hierarchy), leadership (in a particular area of ministry), close mutual collaboration (with bishops, priests, and deacons), and preparation and formation (appropriate to their responsibilities).

Though lay ecclesial ministers are valued for all the good work they do, it is important not to confuse lay ecclesial ministers with the ordained clergy. This is to ensure that the unique vocations of both the clergy and the laity are safeguarded from losing their distinctive characteristics. It is also so that the lay faithful do not lose sight of the importance and the power of the Sacraments, which in general can be administered by the clergy only.

© Bill Wittman/www.wpwittman.com

Because lay Christians are called to be *in* the world but not *of* it, they are able to **evangelize** in a unique way. The laity can bear Christian witness within the many areas of society that are often inaccessible to those, such as the clergy, who have more "official" roles within the Church.

Lay Christians are also able to work to bring secular affairs into alignment with Christian values. For example, a Catholic politician can strive to enact laws that protect human life in all its stages, and a Catholic business owner can help to support families by paying fair salaries. The lay faithful can also glorify God by simply striving for excellence in whatever job they happen to have. A Catholic teacher glorifies God by being the best teacher he or she can be. A Catholic doctor glorifies God by being a good doctor. You can honor and praise God by being a diligent student and by studying and learning to the best of your ability. ✝

apostolate

The Christian person's activity that fulfills the apostolic nature of the whole Church when he or she works to extend the Kingdom of Christ to the entire world. If your school shares the wisdom of its founder, its namesake, or the charism of the religious order that founded it, it is important to learn about this person or order and his or her charism, because as a graduate you will likely want to incorporate this charism into your own apostolate.

evangelize

The action of proclaiming the Good News of Jesus Christ through words and witness.

Article 9 Called to Be Priest, Prophet, and King

Through Baptism we are incorporated into Christ's Body, the Church. Thus we come to a closer identification with Christ, especially by taking part in his sonship as the adopted children of God. All the baptized come to share in Christ's priestly, prophetic, and kingly mission. However, the lay faithful have their own necessary and special way of fulfilling these aspects of their baptismal vocation. One way laypeople are supported in living out their call to be priest, prophet, and king is through participation in parish life.

The water of Baptism is a sign of new life. Water can be poured three times over the head, or the entire body can be immersed three times in a pool of water.

© P Deliss/Godong/Corbis

prophet

A person God chooses to speak his message of salvation. In the Bible, primarily a communicator of a divine message of repentance to the Chosen People, not necessarily a person who predicted the future.

Priest

By virtue of their Baptism, the laity are called to participate in the life of the Trinity by offering every aspect of their lives as a spiritual sacrifice with Christ to the Father, in union with the Holy Spirit. In this way they are fulfilling the priestly aspect of their vocation; that is, every action of their daily lives, no matter how mundane or seemingly insignificant, should be done as a gift to God. Every deed can be made into a praise of God if it is done out of love for him, and laypeople are called to make the constant praise of God, through their thoughts, words, and deeds, a major focus in their lives. Just as an ordained priest offers gifts to God in the holy sacrifice of the Mass, the lay faithful are called to live in such a way that the gift of their lives is likewise offered for the glory of God. Laypeople also share in Christ's priestly mission by participating in the Church's life of prayer, by assisting in some specific ministries of the Church (such as that of lector, choir member, or altar server), and by living a vibrant sacramental life.

Prophet

By virtue of their Baptism, the laity are also called to share in Christ's prophetic mission. A **prophet** is one who speaks for God, conveying God's message to the people and making known the truth about who God is. Laypeople are called to a prophetic vocation in that they are called to serve as witnesses to the saving power of Christ to the world.

Laypeople speak for God and witness in this way by leading lives in accord with Christ's teaching and by demonstrating their firm belief in the mysteries of our faith. For the most part, the laity have the chance to bear a particularly fruitful witness in this regard, as they often encounter unbelievers or non-Christians in their daily life of work or study. Through their Christian way of life, the lay faithful have the chance to introduce Christ to those who may never have had a genuine encounter with Christ or the opportunity to know his Church. They might also collaborate with the hierarchy in specific ministries in their parish or diocese, such as that of catechist or religion teacher.

King

The laity are also called to share in Christ's kingly office through service to others. We can understand this best when we recall that Christ was a servant leader. As the Gospel of Matthew tells us, "[T]he Son of Man did not come to be served but to serve and to give his life as a ransom for many" (20:28). The laity are likewise called to be servant leaders. Servant leadership starts with cultivating self-discipline and consistently choosing what is good and right. It continues with committing to follow God's call with all one's strength and soul. And it includes service to others: family, school, workplace, community, and the larger world. Laypeople are especially called to serve those most in need because, as Christ said, "Whatever you did for one of these least brothers of mine, you did for me" (Matthew 25:40). The laity can also share in Christ's kingly mission by taking on appropriate lay leadership roles in the parish such as membership on parish committees that assist the parish priest. Lay theologians sometimes also serve the hierarchy as consultants in councils and synods.

Serving others is a key part of our baptismal call. How are you of service to other people in your school, parish, or local community?

© Bill Wittman/www.wpwittman.com

Parish Life

A layperson typically lives out his or her baptismal vocation as member of a parish. A parish is a distinct, stable community within a diocese, typically cared for by one or more priests appointed by the bishop.

Live It!

Get Involved!

Think about what you might do to live out your own baptismal vocation within your parish. How can you get involved? No matter what your interests or personality, it is likely that there is some way for you to participate actively in the life of your parish.

For example, does your parish have a youth group you could join? Or maybe you would be interested in serving at Mass as a reader, an altar server, an usher, or a member of the choir. Many parishes have multiple service and outreach opportunities or groups that focus on particular issues of peace and justice. You might also consider volunteering to teach or assist a religious education class for the children of your parish. Whatever your particular interests, your parish will benefit from your involvement, and you may get further insight into the vocation to which God is calling you.

For laypeople the parish is their spiritual home. Members of a parish celebrate the Eucharist together on Sunday and Holy Days, and parishes are places where many of the other Sacraments are celebrated as well. Coming together as a community strengthens one's faith, and the formation of deep friendships with other parishioners can be the source of great support throughout one's life. Parishes often have a variety of groups that parishioners can participate in, such as Bible-study groups and prayer groups. Other groups focus on living one's faith through charitable outreach and justice issues.

A parish community is also responsible for the faith formation of its members. This includes Sacrament preparation for engaged couples about to marry, for the parents of infants to be baptized, for those who will celebrate First Reconciliation and First Holy Communion and Confirmation, and for adults who are becoming Catholic. Parish faith formation efforts also include programs of catechesis, or religious education, for both children and adults. These programs are designed to help people to learn the truths of faith and live as disciples. A parish community also celebrates special events together and usually maintains its own traditions, such as an annual parish picnic or a feast-day festival.

The parish is the basic structural unit of the universal Church. The parishes of a particular geographic region make up a diocese, which is guided by a bishop. In their relationship to the local parish, laypeople participate in the life of the universal, world-wide Catholic Church. ✝

Article 10 The Single Life

Is the single life of a layperson its own vocation? In one sense, the answer would have to be no. The *Catechism of the Catholic Church* does not include lay single life as one of the possible vocational states in life (see 873). And it is true that the lay single life lacks many of the elements that are normally considered a part of a vocation. For example, nobody chooses to enter into the single state of life, as we all start our lives as single people. Unlike marriage, consecrated life, or the priesthood, there are no particular steps to take in order to become single; rather, the opposite is true—we remain single until and unless we take steps toward entering another state in life.

Likewise, the single lay life does not necessarily entail any specific kind of lifelong commitment. Entering into both married and ordained life involves lifelong vows or promises expressed in sacramental celebrations. However, the single lay life does not involve any kind of binding promises.

Unlike the priesthood, consecrated life, and marriage, the single life can be a transitional state. When a person is ordained, consecrated, or married, she or he anticipates remaining in this state for the rest of her or his life. In contrast, young single people generally change their state of life at some point, whether through becoming a spouse in marriage or by receiving Holy Orders or entering into consecrated life. In addition, older single laypeople, even those who might have at some point thought that God wanted them to remain single, might choose to marry.

On the other hand, some laypeople are called by God to live out their Christian vocation permanently as single people. Single life that involves a personal consecration or commitment to a permanent, celibate gift of self to God and neighbor can be considered a vocation.

Who Is Called to Be Single?

A man or woman may choose to remain single because he or she has a sense that this is the will of God for him or her in a special way. A person may sense a call to love God with

© Karen Kasmauski/Corbis

an undivided heart by choosing to remain single for the sake of Christ while not entering a formal religious community.

Some people choose a permanent commitment to single life if they have discerned a call to a full-time mission that would make it difficult to live out any other state of life at the same time. For example, a

A Single Saint

Blessed Pier Giorgio Frassati was born in 1901 in Turin, Italy, to a wealthy and politically influential family. Although his parents were Catholic, they were generally lax about the practice of their faith. However, this did nothing to cool Pier Giorgio's love of Christ, especially Christ as seen in the poor and as present in the Eucharist.

In his short life, Pier Giorgio was known for his great devotion to prayer and his tremendous love for the poor. He would often provide for the poor out of his own necessities, at times giving the shoes off his feet or the coat off his back to someone whom he felt needed it more than he did.

Yet at the same time, Pier Giorgio was a "regular guy" who loved being outdoors, spending time with his friends, and even playing practical jokes on people. Although it was often difficult for him, he studied diligently at university. As a layman, he also concerned himself with Catholic social justice issues.

Blessed Pier Giorgio died on July 4, 1925, at the young age of twenty-four, from an illness he is believed to have acquired while performing charitable service in caring for the sick. To the astonishment of his family, who did not know the extent of his acts of service and mercy, his funeral was packed with mourners from among the poor whom he had served.

Today Blessed Pier Giorgio Frassati is an excellent role model for single Catholics, as his life demonstrated how one can combine a vibrant Catholic faith with a joyous human experience of life. Many Catholic singles groups take Blessed Pier Giorgio as their patron.

young Catholic might feel called to go to medical school and become a doctor who travels to foreign countries in order to provide healthcare to the poorest of the poor. The travel, time, and, sometimes, the risks to personal safety involved in such missions can make other states of life more difficult.

spiritual director
A priest or other person who is experienced and knowledgeable about faith, prayer, and spirituality and helps others to grow in their relationship with God.

Other Catholics might feel called to committed single life because they have serious responsibilities to which they must attend. For instance, a single lay Catholic might have the obligation of caring for elderly parents or a disabled sibling. Though caring for a parent or sibling does not necessarily preclude another vocation, it may be that the single person comes to understand that these life circumstances in fact reveal his or her particular call for serving others and the Church.

Whatever the particular reason for choosing to live a committed, single life, it is important to note that this state of life can be very fulfilling and important to the mission of the Church. As with all vocations, it is helpful for those who are considering a call to live the single lay life to discern this with a mentor or **spiritual director.**

What Do Single People Do?

Single people live out their Christian vocation in a wide variety of ways, depending on their gifts, interests, careers, and abilities. Like all Catholics, single laypeople are called to live the fullness of Christian discipleship. By their Baptism single laypeople are called to live lives of virtue and friendship with God. Like all of the baptized, single laypeople are encouraged to make the Sacraments an integral part of their lives,

Catholic Wisdom

Single but Complete

In her book *The Thrill of the Chaste*, Dawn Eden writes about her experiences as a single woman newly committed to a life of chastity: "A woman with the courage to step out into the unknown, risking temporary loneliness for a shot at lasting joy, is more than a 'single.' She's *singular*. Instead of defining herself by what she lacks—a relationship with a man—she defines herself by what she has: a relationship with God" (page 22).

All single people, male and female, can find joy in their state in life if they define it according to their relationship with God.

especially the Sacraments of Penance and Reconciliation and the Eucharist.

Because the single lay life entails more personal freedom than any other state of life within the Church, single laypeople are often able to participate in parish life or in the Church's charitable mission more fully than those who are married. Single laypeople often have more time to visit the sick, feed the poor, teach the truths of the faith to others, and participate in various facets of parish life. ✝

Part Review

1. Who are the lay faithful?

2. What do we mean when we say that the laity have a vocation to be *in* the world but not *of* the world?

3. What does it mean to share in Christ's priestly, prophetic, and kingly mission?

4. Why is the parish important to laypeople?

5. In what sense can the single life be considered a vocation?

6. What are some signs or situations that could indicate that a lay Catholic may be called to remain single?

Married Life

Part 1

Understanding Christian Marriage

Most Catholics will be called to serve God and his Church through the vocation of married life. Marriage is a lifelong covenant, modeled on that between Christ and the Church. In marriage a baptized man and a baptized woman make an exclusive and permanent commitment to faithfully love each other and to cooperate in the procreation and education of children.

Marriage can be understood on a number of different levels. Every culture in history has acknowledged the importance of marriage in one way or another, making marriage a universal part of the human experience. Marriage also benefits civil society in a number of important ways.

On a deeper, more significant level, we can appreciate marriage as a part of God's plan for creation. Marriage is an institution created by God for the good of the human race.

Finally, because Christ gave human marriage the dignity of being a Sacrament, the vocation of married life has become a special source of grace for spouses and a privileged way for men and women to encounter God's love. The Sacrament of Matrimony also serves to remind the whole Church of God's love for his people.

The articles in this part address the following topics:

Article 11 God, the Author of Marriage

Think of some of the institutions or organizations that human beings create, such as schools, clubs, teams, professional associations, and governments. One thing all of these institutions or organizations have in common is that it is up to humans themselves to define what they are and how they are structured.

If you were to set up your own club, you would be free to determine your club's nature and purpose. You could decide for yourself what your club would be about, what kind of activities you would undertake, who could join your club, and how someone might become a member. Governments too are free to name their own foundational principles, to choose their own means for appointing authority, and to write their own laws. In the case of purely human institutions, those establishing the institutions can legitimately create systems according to whatever they believe works best.

In the case of marriage, however, this principle cannot apply, because although marriage is a reality of human life and an institution into which humans enter, marriage is not a purely human institution. Rather, God himself is the author of marriage.

The exchange of rings is a sign of a couple's love of and fidelity to each other.

© Bill Wittman/www.wpwittman.com

What Is Marriage?

Marriage, or Matrimony, is a Sacrament at the Service of Communion. This means that it is a Sacrament that promotes the salvation of others and serves to build up the Church. (Holy Orders is the other Sacrament at the Service of Communion and is the subject of section 3 of this book.) Marriage is the faithful, lifelong union of a baptized man and a baptized woman committed to loving each other forever and being open to the gift of children. In marriage the husband and wife make a free and total commitment of their entire lives to each other. They pledge their hearts, minds, bodies, and resources to each other in an exclusive and lasting way, welcoming and educating whatever children God gives to them.

The Church's Teaching on Homosexuality

Marriage is always between one man and one woman. This is a truth that is informed by **natural law**. Marriage requires the genuine emotional and sexual complementarity found only between a man and a woman, because only the sexual act between a man and a woman can result in new life—one of the purposes of marriage. Thus, it is not possible to redefine marriage to include homosexual unions.

Those with a homosexual orientation deserve love and respect as human beings created in the image and likeness of God. Because men and women who experience same-sex attraction are endowed with the same fundamental dignity as all human beings, the Church vehemently opposes any violence, hatred, or discrimination toward those who identify themselves as gay or lesbian. Furthermore, a homosexual *orientation* is not considered a sin. Homosexual *acts*, however, are sinful because they are not open to the possibility of life and are therefore contrary to natural law and to what is written into the body itself.

Like all Christians, men and women who experience same-sex attraction are called to a life of chastity. Sexuality is more than just physical expression of sexual attraction—it concerns one's inmost being. Thus, chastity means physically and spiritually integrating one's sexuality within oneself (see *Catechism*, 2337). By living a life of chastity and virtue, those with a homosexual orientation can attain perfection in charity and live the fullness of the Christian life.

For those who realize they are sexually attracted to people of the same sex, this inclination and the call to chastity can be a cross to bear, requiring great effort at mastering will over emotions. An active prayer life, regular participation in the Sacraments of the Eucharist and Penance and Reconciliation, and support from the faith community can help men and women with homosexual inclinations to live faithful Christian lives filled with loving relationships among family and friends.

Marriage Points toward God

Throughout history every society has, in at least some sense, recognized the value of marriage. In fact, the very well-being of societies and their individual members is closely related to the health of marriage and family life. Societies may not always celebrate marriage in the same way or see it as meaning exactly the same thing, but the greatness of the union of man and woman is indeed recognized throughout the world. This is due to the fact that the vocation of marriage is part of the very nature of created man and woman.

Though marriage should be valued and cherished for its contribution to society, we know that marriage has an even deeper significance. It is beyond a purely human institution. Marriage points us toward God and is rooted in him. Because we were created by God out of love, we were also created *for* love. This, in fact, can be seen as a core understanding of what it means to be a human person. The love that a man and woman share, which is celebrated in the Sacrament of Matrimony, provides us with an image of the very love that God unfailingly has for human beings.

Because marriage was created by God, following his plan for marriage will bring us closer to him. The love between a husband and wife serves to remind the whole Church of the love God has for his people. The intimate communion of life and love that characterizes Christian marriage is a sign and symbol of God's covenant with his people, a covenant of love and grace in Jesus Christ. It also models to others the love and mutual self-giving that is the mark of Christian activity in society and in the Church. ✝

natural law
The moral law that can be understood through our intellect and the use of reason. It is our God-given instinct to be in right relationship with God, other people, the world, and ourselves. The basis for natural law is our participation in God's wisdom and goodness because we are created in the divine likeness.

Catholic Wisdom

Marriage and the Good of Society

In the *Pastoral Constitution on the Church in the Modern World (Gaudium et Spes)*, the bishops of Vatican II write about the nature of marriage:

> For God himself is the author of marriage and has endowed it with various values and purposes: all of these have a very important bearing on the continuation of the human race, on the personal development and eternal destiny of every member of the family, on the dignity, stability, peace, and prosperity of the family and of the whole human race. (48)

Article 12 Marriage in the Old Testament

Although the institution of marriage can be understood and appreciated by even the most secular of societies, this does not change the fact that marriage was specifically planned and designed by God. The Old Testament is one place where we can clearly learn about God's plan for marriage. Here we read about God's creation of human beings and marriage, how the marriage covenant helps to protect us from the effects of Original Sin, the fact that marriage is the source of many blessings, and the ways in which marriage can serve as a means for coming to understand God more fully.

The Creation of Humans

God established the institution of marriage from almost the very beginning of creation. In the Creation account in the first chapter of the Book of Genesis, we read the following:

This image of Adam and Eve is taken from a fresco at the Monastery of Saint-Antoine-le-Grand in France.

© Pascal Deloche/Godong/Corbis

God created mankind in his image;
    in the image of God he created them;
    male and female he created them.
God blessed them and God said to them: Be fertile and multiply; fill the earth and subdue it.

(Genesis 1:27–28)

This passage helps us to understand that marriage was a part of God's plan from the very beginning. Men and women were to join together to be cocreators with God, filling the earth with their descendants, made in the image and likeness of God just as the first man and woman themselves were.

In the second Creation account in Genesis, we are given a much more detailed account of the first instance of the human vocation to marriage:

It is not good for the man to be alone. I will make a helper suited to him. So the Lord God formed out of the ground all the wild animals and all the birds of the air . . . but none proved to be a helper suited to the man.

So the LORD God cast a deep sleep on the man, and while he was asleep, he took out one of his ribs and closed up its place with flesh. The LORD God then built the rib that he had taken from the man into a woman. When he brought her to the man, the man said:
"This one, at last, is bone of my bones
      and flesh of my flesh. . . ."
That is why a man leaves his father and mother and clings to his wife, and the two of them become one body.

                                                   (Genesis 2:18–24)

wisdom literature
The Old Testament Books of Proverbs, Job, Ecclesiastes, Sirach, and the Wisdom of Solomon.

Sin, Justice, and the Law

The Paradise that Adam and Eve once enjoyed became off-limits to them after the Fall when they first disobeyed God. With the consequences of Original Sin upon them, marriage—initially a relationship of perfect harmony and love—became subject to various forms of corruption and weakness. Some consequences of Original Sin named in the book of Genesis are pain in childbirth and hard toil in work.

When God gave Moses the Law as described in the Book of Exodus (see 20:11–17), the many legal restrictions centered around marriage were meant as a way to protect against the effects of Original Sin. Husbands were required by the Law to treat their wives fairly, and adultery was forbidden. Because the Law held marriage to be a covenant and a sacred institution, men and women were required to strive to overcome their sinful tendencies for the good of each other as well as for the good of the community.

Source of Abundant Blessings

We can learn more about the marriage covenant in the Old Testament from the **wisdom literature**. The view of marriage and family life found in wisdom literature is wonderfully positive in its emphasis on the essential goodness of marriage and childrearing. Marriage and children are portrayed first and foremost as precious gifts from God and as the source of great joy.

For example, in the Book of Proverbs, we find this description of the value of a good wife:

Who can find a woman of worth?
      Far beyond jewels is her value.

> Her husband trusts her judgment;
>> he does not lack income.
> She brings him profit, not loss,
>> all the days of her life.
>
> (31:10–12)

This description is echoed in the Book of Sirach:

> Happy the husband of a good wife;
>> the number of his days will be doubled.
> A loyal wife brings joy to her husband,
>> and he will finish his years in peace.
> A good wife is a generous gift
>> bestowed upon him who fears the Lord.
> Whether rich or poor, his heart is content,
>> a smile ever on his face.
>
> (26:1–4)

Many of the Psalms proclaim the joys of bearing children. Psalm 127 states the following:

> Certainly sons are a gift from the LORD,
>> the fruit of the womb, a reward.
> Like arrows in the hand of a warrior
>> are the sons born in one's youth.
> Blessed is the man who has filled his quiver with them.
> He will never be shamed
>> for he will destroy his foes at the gate.
>
> (Verses 3–5)

Live It!

The Song of Songs

One of the most complex books of the Old Testament, the Song of Songs, can be interpreted from many perspectives—allegorical, cultic, dramatic, and literal. Traditionally, the lover and the beloved in this book are interpreted as standing for Israel and God, or for Jesus and the Church.

The Church looks at the unique expression of human love in these poems as a reflection of divine love. The passion and beauty expressed are a reflection of the passion and beauty of God's love for us. So too the mutual love shared in marriage is an image of the love that God has for all of his people.

To adequately express our love in any relationship, we need to have dialogue. Open and honest communication provides the basis for maintaining and deepening the bonds of respect, friendship, and love. What steps can you take to have open and honest communication in the relationships in your life?

The Prophets: God's Fidelity to Israel

The prophets of the Old Testament were given a special vocation by God to speak to the people of Israel on his behalf. They often called the Israelites to a spirit of repentance, preaching God's displeasure with his people's social injustices as well as their frequent lapses into **idolatry**.

idolatry
The worship of false gods in violation of the First Commandment.

One theme that runs throughout the prophets' writings is the image of God's being married to his people. The idolatry of the Israelites is compared to the sin of adultery. However, God is the ever-faithful husband who is always anxious to forgive his bride and to take her back to himself.

Here is an example from the Book of Isaiah:

> For your husband is your Maker;
> > the LORD of hosts is his name,
> Your redeemer, the Holy One of Israel,
> > called God of all the earth.

> The LORD calls you back,
> > like a wife forsaken and grieved in spirit,
> A wife married in youth and then cast off,
> > says your God.
> For a brief moment I abandoned you,
> > but with great tenderness I will take you back.
> > > (54:5–7)

Similarly, the entire book of Hosea deals with the themes of repentance and renewed fidelity. Hosea's unconditional love of his wife—even in the face of her infidelity—reflects God's love and continued longing for Israel, despite the nation's transgressions.

In the second chapter of Hosea, we read God's message to Israel as conveyed to the prophet. Here, God expresses his desire to reunite with Israel in a renewed bond of marital faithfulness:

> Therefore, I will allure her now;
> > I will lead her into the wilderness
> > and speak persuasively to her. . . .

> I will betroth you to me forever:
> > I will betroth you to me with justice and with judgment,
> > with loyalty and with compassion;
> I will betroth you to me with fidelity,

and you shall know the LORD.
(Verses 16,21–22)

covenant
A personal, solemn promise of faithful love that involves mutual commitments and creates a sacred relationship.

The image of God's being married to his people in the prophets' writings is a recurring theme and one that shows us God's great love for us. Through these writings we see that God is ever faithful and always ready to forgive us. We also come to understand that marriage itself is a beautiful image for the unending love that God has for us. ✝

Covenant versus Contract

The Old Testament portrays marriage—as well as God's relationship to Israel—as a **covenant** rather than as simply a legal contract. But you may be wondering, what is the difference between the two terms?

Usually a contract is an agreement that involves an exchange of goods or services. For example, contracts are written today for people buying or selling a major item, such as a house or car. Other contracts may involve a certain kind of work one party will provide for another, such as the construction work for a new building, which is performed for an agreed-upon price.

A covenant is an agreement that goes much deeper than an exchange of goods. A covenant can be considered an exchange of persons. Those who enter into a covenant promise their very selves to each other. Marriage can be seen as a covenant because in it a man and a woman promise to remain faithful to each other until death. God's "marriage" to Israel is a covenant, because God promises his special loving concern for the nation of Israel in exchange for Israel's wholehearted fidelity to the one true God.

13 Marriage in the New Testament

Article

One of the keys for understanding Scripture is to see the many ways in which the New Testament is a fulfillment of all the promises made by God in the Old Testament. God's laws in the Old Testament are not canceled in the New Testament but are given an even deeper significance.

This is also true in the case of marriage. In the Old Testament, marriage was a sacred covenant created and blessed by God. In the New Testament, marriage is given the additional dignity of numbering among the Seven Sacraments.

The Wedding at Cana

Marriage is one of the Seven Sacraments, all of which were instituted by Christ. Although marriage existed before the coming of Jesus Christ in the Incarnation, Jesus affirmed the goodness of marriage and raised it to the dignity of a Sacrament at the time of his first miracle during the changing of water into wine at the wedding feast at Cana (see John 2:1–10).

© The Gallery Collection/Corbis

An early nineteenth-century painting titled "The Marriage at Cana."

Though the bride and groom at the wedding at Cana were undoubtedly grateful that Jesus stepped in to save them from social embarrassment at their wedding reception, the significance of Jesus' action here goes much deeper than simply keeping a party afloat. This was Jesus' first public sign or miracle—that is, the first place where he openly manifested his identity as the Incarnate Son of God.

By choosing to reveal himself as God at a wedding, Jesus was also showing us the value of marriage. And just as water—something good in its own right—was changed into the more remarkable substance of wine, so also would the vocation of marriage be raised and transformed into a sign of Christ's presence and a privileged means of encountering God.

The Unity of Marriage

Pharisees

A Jewish sect at the time of Jesus known for its strict adherence to the Law.

Christ established the Sacrament of Matrimony as a union that is absolutely and unquestionably permanent. According to the laws of the Old Testament, a Jewish man could divorce his wife under some conditions; however, Jesus set a higher standard for his followers. Christians were to accept marriage as it was intended by God as a bond that could be broken by only the death of one of the spouses.

We can see this teaching in a conversation Jesus had with the **Pharisees** in the Gospel of Matthew:

> [Jesus] said in reply, "Have you not read that from the beginning the Creator 'made them male and female' and said, 'For this reason a man shall leave his father and mother and be joined to his wife, and the two shall become one flesh'? . . . Therefore, what God has joined together, no human being must separate. . . . Because of the hardness of your hearts Moses allowed you to divorce your wives, but from the beginning it was not so. I say to you, whoever divorces his wife (unless the marriage is unlawful) and marries another commits adultery." (19:4–9)

Christ presents this vision of marriage as the norm according to God's plan. Because Jesus came to free us from Original Sin, we would receive the grace necessary to live

Pray It!

Anniversary Prayer

Just like weddings, anniversaries are times to pray and rejoice. Here is a prayer you can pray for your parents or other couples you know who are celebrating an anniversary:

Dear God,

Bless _____ and _____ on their anniversary.

In their love for each other, they reveal your love to the world.

Give them the grace to live out their marriage covenant, provide them with strength when times are hard, and shower them with joy in the company of family and friends.

Open their eyes to the gifts you have given them in order to serve you by serving others.

May they enjoy many more years together, growing closer to each other and to you.

May they love and honor each other all the days of their lives.

Amen.

married lives that are closer to God's plan for marriage before the Fall.

The Wedding of the Lamb

Another unique aspect of the New Testament's vision of marriage is the way marriage reflects the relationship of Christ to the Church. Many New Testament passages describe the **nuptial** relationship between Christ and his Church.

In his Letter to the Ephesians, Saint Paul sets out a theology of the vocation of married life based on the Church's identity as the Bride of Christ (see Ephesians, chapter 5). In the Book of Revelation, traditionally attributed to Saint John the Apostle, the Church is frequently described as the

nuptial
Something related to marriage or a marriage ceremony.

The Letter to the Ephesians

The same power that unites Christ and the Church also unites a wife and husband. This is what Saint Paul meant in his Letter to the Ephesians:

© Monkey Business Images/Shutterstock.com

> Husbands, love your wives, even as Christ loved the church and handed himself over for her. . . . So husbands should love their wives as their own bodies. . . . For no one hates his own flesh but rather nourishes and cherishes it, even as Christ does the church, because we are members of his body. . . . This is a great mystery, but I speak in reference to Christ and the church. (5:25–32)

Thus the Bible teaches us that the Sacrament of Matrimony signifies the union of Christ and the Church. The permanent nature of the marriage union symbolizes God's unending love for all humanity. The Sacrament gives a husband and wife the grace to love each other as Christ loves the Church. It promotes their dignity, strengthens their unity, makes them a sign of God's love in the world, and helps the couple to perfect their holiness on their journey to eternal life.

spotless Bride of Christ, the Lamb of God. In Revelation 19:7, John has a vision of the heavenly host joyfully singing of the Church: "For the wedding day of the Lamb has come, / his bride has made herself ready." Toward the conclusion of that same vision, John sees the Church, "a new Jerusalem, coming down out of heaven from God, prepared as a bride adorned for her husband" (21:2).

In the New Testament, marriage is not only a covenant and a Sacrament, but also a key analogy for understanding God's love for us. Although the relationship between Christ and the Church is ultimately too profound for us to fully comprehend, we can grasp its nature in a real sense by considering the vocation of married life. When a husband and wife love each other in a total, faithful, fruitful, self-sacrificial, and unconditional way, they are a living reflection of the great love Christ has for his Church. ✝

Part Review

1. What is Christian marriage?

2. Why is it impossible to reinterpret or redefine marriage?

3. What are some of the things we can learn about marriage from reading the Old Testament?

4. Why is marriage a covenant rather than a contract?

5. In what sense is Christian marriage unique?

6. Explain how marriage reflects Christ's love for his Church.

Part 2

Preparing for Marriage

When does preparation for marriage begin? This may seem like a trick question when we consider that preparation for marriage happens in three stages.

Preparation for marriage begins in our childhood as we learn basic concepts of love and respect. We usually gain our first ideas about marriage from our family. Ideally, the home where we grow up is also where we gain the qualities necessary to relate well to others, including a future spouse.

The next stage of preparation occurs when we are teens and young adults. As we move from childhood to adolescence and early adulthood, we start to consider marriage in a more mature way—that is, we begin to envision it as a serious possibility for us. Your teenage and young adult years are an excellent time to become more educated on the Church's teachings on marriage and family life.

Engaged couples take part in a third and final stage of immediate preparation for marriage. This stage includes participating in special marriage preparation programs offered through the parish or diocese as well as planning the wedding liturgy.

The articles in this part address the following topics:

^{Article}14 Grounded in Respect

Preparation for marriage begins years before a vocation to married life seriously enters our minds. It begins early in our childhood as we grow in awareness of who we are and what kind of people we should be.

During this stage of life, through the examples and lessons gained by interacting with parents, relatives, and others, we begin to understand who we are and what it means to be in relationship with other people. Through spiritual and catechetical formation, we begin to understand married life as a vocation. We also begin to learn to respect ourselves and others by behaving in ways and fostering attitudes that acknowledge that all human persons, men and women, are loved by God and have inherent dignity as beings created in his image and likeness. These are all key skills that become part of our first preparation for the lifelong commitment of marriage.

© wavebreakmedia ltd/Shutterstock.com

Who are positive examples in your life that help you understand what it means to be in loving relationship with other people?

Social Skills

One way we learn who we are and what it means to be in relationship with others is by developing good social skills. Social skills are attitudes, habits, and disciplines that enable us to relate to our fellow human beings in a loving and respectful way. Social skills encompass such concepts as good manners, common courtesy, and friendliness.

Consider the following social skills that are necessary to build good relationships. In which areas do you have strengths, and in which areas might you have weaknesses?

- **Personal maturity:** Do you take responsibility for your own choices and mistakes?

- **Reliability:** Do you keep your promises? Do you show up when you say you will? Do you meet your responsibilities (like homework or chores) in a timely and conscientious way?

- **Respect:** Do you treat others the way you want to be treated? Do you recognize that others' needs, wants, and opinions are just as important as your own? Do you strive to see the image and likeness of God in everyone you meet? Do you show the proper deference to those in authority, such as your parents and teachers?

- **Courtesy:** Do you try to make other people feel welcome and at ease? Do you treat others with kindness?

- **Fortitude and perseverance:** Do you stand up for what is right even if doing so is difficult? Do you follow through on your commitments, even when circumstances get challenging?

- **Prudence or common sense:** Do you strive to discern the wisest course of action?

- **Communication:** Can you express yourself clearly in a confident yet respectful manner? Are you a good listener who cares about what others have to say?

family of origin
The family in which one was raised as a child. Families of origin can include parents, siblings, extended family members, or others who played a significant role in one's childhood and youth.

These interpersonal skills will serve you well throughout your life, in whatever vocation God calls you to embrace. They are important in marriage because marriage is not just a call to relate to another person but a call to share one's whole life with another.

How has your family of origin formed who you are and how you relate to the world?

Families of Origin

Your **family of origin** is the family in which you have been raised. Parents and siblings usually form one's family of origin, but it may also include grandparents, extended family members, or others who have been a big part of one's childhood.

Your family of origin is important because it forms who you are and how you relate to the world. If parents show respect to their spouse and children, their children will naturally absorb and exhibit the same respectful attitude. Likewise, the way parents and other

© wong sze yuen/Shutterstock.com

close married couples relate to and treat each other informs children's understanding of what it means to be married.

Even household rules have the potential to influence what kind of adults children will become. For instance, if your parents have a strict "no fighting with siblings" rule, you may develop a strong ability to solve conflicts through compromise and mutual communication.

Our families of origin also affect our spirituality. Growing up with a caring and loving father figure helps us relate to God the Father. A warm and nurturing mother can help us to understand how God always loves his people. A stable home life, in which we can always count on our parents to be there for us, teaches us how to trust both God and others and how to be trustworthy in turn.

However, no family is perfect. All families have flaws and weak points. Some families have more problems than others; occasionally families will have serious problems that may require outside intervention, such as counseling. And just as our families' strong points can shape our personalities for the better, our families' flaws can develop areas of our lives that need healing.

No matter what problems we experience in our families, it is important to understand that such difficulties do not automatically determine who we will become. If we are aware of the areas of our lives that need particular attention and healing as a result of family issues, we can take steps to deal with them and recover from them. Part of becoming an adult is taking personal responsibility for what kind of people we are. It is completely possible to overcome nega-

Catholic Wisdom

Pope Saint John Paul II on the Mission of the Family

Family life has its own special mission within the Church. As pope, Saint John Paul II wrote about this mission in his document *On the Role of the Christian Family in the Modern World (Familiaris Consortio)*:

The family has the mission to become more and more what it is, that is to say, a community of life and love. . . . Hence the family has the mission to guard, reveal and communicate love, and this is a living reflection of and a real sharing in God's love for humanity and the love of Christ the Lord for the Church His bride. (17)

A Family of Faith

In October 2001, Pope Saint John Paul II beatified Luigi Quattrocchi (1880–1951) and Maria Beltrame Quattrocchi (1884–1965), an Italian couple that was married for forty-six years. Luigi and Maria had four children. The Quattrocchi family was busy and active in the world around them. Maria wrote books on the mother's role in the education of her children. She accompanied sick people on pilgrimages to Lourdes, in France. Luigi was a lawyer and worked for the Italian government. He was an active participant in several Catholic organizations. Every day this family prayed the Rosary together and shared a devotion to the Eucharist.

The Quattrocchis knew what it meant to live in modern times, with the threats of war, disease, and poverty. The family worked to help Jewish people escape Nazi persecution in Italy. Their lives were an expression of their love for one another and their deep faith. This Italian family of our time reminds us of Jesus' family of ancient times. Both families are models for us today. The Quattrocchis' feast day is November 28.

tive effects from childhood. In fact, chances are that some of the adults you admire and may consider as role models have overcome difficult situations and problems they experienced in their home lives when they were children or teens.

As you consider whether married life may be the vocation to which God is calling you, it is helpful to spend some time reflecting on how experiences you had growing up might affect your attitude toward marriage and to identify negative experiences or learning that you will have to overcome. ✝

Article 15 Preparation for a Lifelong Commitment

The next stage of preparation for marriage is called proximate preparation. The word *proximate* means "near." This stage of preparation typically takes place during the adolescent and young adult years, when a person begins to consider the vocation of married life in a more adult way, even if he or she does not have any immediate plans to marry.

Proximate preparation happens through education, both in terms of more formal instruction and learning as well as through formative life experiences. In fact, this section of this text can be seen as part of the proximate preparation for marriage.

In this stage of preparation, it is important that a variety of issues related to marriage are covered and more fully understood. Some issues that are important at this time of education include learning about ourselves and the role that human sexuality plays in our lives. This period of preparation should also include an understanding of God's intentions in creating men and women who naturally complement each other, of how marriage promotes the dignity of both men and women, and of how sexual intimacy is meant to be saved for marriage.

It is important that we learn about the skills that are necessary for living a lifelong commitment, including the giving of oneself to one's spouse. We must understand that marriage requires many things of us, including discipline, generosity, and fully understanding the meaning of love.

Live It!

Ten Ways to Practice Chastity

1. Pray. Thank God for the gift of sexuality, and ask for the strength to live a life of chastity.
2. Seek out a parent or another adult you can talk to when you have questions about sexuality.
3. Focus on making friends with people of the opposite sex.
4. Learn to turn a critical eye toward media messages that use sex to sell products.
5. Remind yourself that your value does not depend on whether or how much you date.
6. Stay away from drugs and alcohol. Impaired judgment on a date could lead to trouble.
7. If you are on a date and things get out of hand, call a friend or a parent for a ride home.
8. If you have a boyfriend or a girlfriend, communicate openly and set boundaries about touching.
9. Remember that more teenagers are *not* having sex than *are* having sex.
10. Make a pledge to avoid intimate sexual activity until you get married.

Understanding and developing healthy relationships is an important part of this stage of preparation.

The Virtue of Chastity

Coming to a deeper and richer understanding of the virtue of **chastity** is one important element for forming healthy relationships within our life of faith. Chastity is the virtue by which people healthfully integrate their sexuality into their total person.

> **chastity**
> The virtue by which people are able to successfully and healthfully integrate their sexuality into their total person; recognized as one of the fruits of the Holy Spirit.

The virtue of chastity is lived in different ways in different states of life. For married people, chastity means experiencing sexual intimacy only with one's spouse and no other. Marital chastity also includes being open to new life in every instance of sexual union. Unmarried men and women, in contrast, live the virtue of chastity by abstaining from sexual acts.

We all have a serious responsibility to live the virtue of chastity. Deliberate unchaste acts, committed in full knowledge that they are wrong, are grave sins. Sins against chastity, such as premarital sex and cohabitation, do serious damage to our relationship with God, each other, and ourselves, and they implicitly encourage others to devalue chastity and the sacredness of marriage.

But we must realize that chastity, when practiced with a generous heart, is a beautiful and powerful virtue, not a limitation. Chastity allows us to be whole in our identity and at peace with who we are, and it is a powerful aid as we strive to become who God created us to be. When we are chaste, we acknowledge that our bodies are, in the words of Saint Paul, "temple[s] of the holy Spirit" (1 Corinthians 6:19).

Chastity is primarily a matter of love. When we are chaste, our love for God and for others can become more pure, more profound, and more selfless.

Dating can be a part of the preparation process for marriage. What elements and qualities do you think are essential for a healthy dating relationship?

© auremar/Shutterstock.com

Dating

Another element of proximate preparation for marriage is learning about healthy personal and dating habits. Dating can help us to get to know someone better, learn what qualities we might look for in a future spouse,

and continue to develop the social skills needed to sustain a loving relationship. Dating in high school and college is one way to learn firsthand about the importance of communication and the value of considering others' needs and desires as well as our own. It can also help us to discern whether we might, indeed, have a vocation to married life.

Dating should always be built on the solid principles of basic friendship. We sometimes hear stories of young men and women who started out as just friends, but whose relationship eventually developed into something more. Still, even for couples who first came to know each other through dating, real friendship must form the foundation of their romantic feelings for each other.

Real friendship allows us to feel comfortable being ourselves around another person. Friends also care about each other for who they are, instead of just how they make each other feel. Friends usually have common interests and genuinely enjoy each other's company. It is important for dating couples to be friends, because their friendship will help them to care about each other in a deeper and more real way. And if they begin to fall in love, a foundation of friendship will promote a genuine, selfless love that more closely witnesses to the love of Christ and the Church.

In any relationship, respecting each other's boundaries is important. In a dating relationship, this especially includes respecting physical and moral boundaries. Dating couples, like all Christians, are called to practice the virtue of chastity, and because they are unmarried, they must refrain from sexual intimacy.

To maintain chaste physical boundaries in a dating relationship, the most effective question is not, How far can I go before I cross the line? but rather, What do I need to do to have a chaste relationship? Always keep in mind that remaining chaste, and helping your boyfriend or girlfriend to do the same, is the most loving thing you can do for each other.

Appropriate emotional boundaries are also important. Dating is not marriage but merely a step that can lead to marriage. Dating is essentially a process of discernment, and dating couples should give each other the freedom to continue listening for God's will, even if God does not will that the couple should be together for life. ✝

Choosing a Spouse

How can you recognize when you have found a good potential husband or wife? First, it is important to keep in mind that there is no such thing as a perfect spouse; even the best husband or wife for you will never be 100 percent perfect.

If you believe that marriage is your vocation, think about the personal qualities that are most important to you in a person with whom you will spend the rest of your life. For example, would you have a hard time spending your life with a spouse who was not a good listener? Maybe you feel that you would need to be married to someone with a good sense of humor to navigate life's day-to-day challenges. Perhaps you consider it essential that your future spouse will share your views on politics, money management, raising children, or the importance of spending time with extended family.

Whatever personal traits you consider necessary, any prospective spouse needs to demonstrate some essential qualities in order for a loving, healthy marriage to develop. Without exception, a potential spouse should be someone who is respectful. This means that he or she takes your feelings into consideration and avoids hurtful comments. Of course, you should *never* marry anyone who would abuse you physically or emotionally.

A potential spouse should also share your values, especially your faith and your beliefs about the nature of marriage. Accordingly, a suitable partner would also honor and share your commitment to chastity.

Finally, one other quality you should always seek in a future spouse is trustworthiness. A prospective partner should be someone who keeps his or her word, someone on whom you can depend. A potential husband or wife should be someone whom you could trust with your life, because that is exactly what you do when you agree to marry someone.

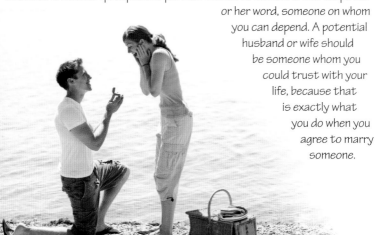

^{Article}16 Immediate Preparation

Today the phrase "wedding planning" calls to mind all the practical chores involved in preparing for the wedding celebration—finding the right dress, caterer, florist, and photographer; choosing the bridal party; sending out invitations; and tending to the countless details that go into ensuring an enjoyable and joy-filled celebration. A lot of work goes into making a wedding and reception a beautiful occasion. This is not necessarily bad, because marriage is an important event in a couple's life that deserves to be celebrated.

However, we know that all of these planning details are secondary to preparing for the Sacrament of Matrimony itself. The most important part of a bride and bridegroom's wedding day is the celebration of the Rite of Marriage, which takes place in church, ordinarily as part of a Mass. Because the Eucharist is at the center of our lives as Catholics, it only makes sense that it would be at the forefront of one of the most important days of a couple's life.

Meeting with the Priest

Once a couple is engaged, the first step in planning a Catholic wedding is usually to meet with the priest (or in some cases the deacon) who will celebrate the nuptial liturgy. Often the priest is the pastor of the bride or bridegroom's parish. The purpose of this initial meeting is for the priest to begin guiding the couple toward a deeper understanding of the Sacrament of Matrimony.

The priest invites the engaged couple to share the story of how they met, why they decided to get married, and what marriage means to them. The couple also has the opportunity to bring up any questions about the Church's teachings on marriage or whatever concerns they might have about their own

readiness to marry. If the couple does not clearly understand some aspects of what marriage entails, the priest may give them guidance or instruction on these points.

Setting a Date

If both the priest and the couple believe that the couple is ready to begin to prepare for the Sacrament of Matrimony, they can schedule a wedding date on the parish calendar. Many dioceses in the United States have a standard policy that weddings must be scheduled at least six months in advance.

Six months may seem like a long time for a couple to wait, but this time serves several purposes. First, it ensures that the couple has adequate time to learn more about the Church's teaching on marriage and to consider their decision to marry—a six-month wait can prevent couples from rushing into a lifelong commitment without considering its seriousness. Second, this waiting period gives the priest and the couple time to gather the paperwork required to ensure that the marriage will be valid in the Church. For example, the bride and the bridegroom will both need to request new baptismal certificates, and some couples may even need to receive special permission or a **dispensation** from the local bishop, such as when a Catholic seeks to marry a non-Catholic. Finally, a period of waiting gives the engaged couple time to ready themselves spiritually for the life-changing Sacrament they are looking forward to receiving.

Pre-Cana Preparation

The Church has a responsibility to ensure that engaged couples are suitably prepared for the Sacrament of Matrimony. During the waiting period after a date is set, the engaged couple is required to participate in a marriage preparation program, often called Pre-Cana after the site of Jesus' miracle at the wedding feast at Cana. Depending on the parish or diocese, an engaged couple might attend classes at their parish, or they might take part in a retreat or days of reflection with other engaged couples from around the diocese. Some parishes have programs that match married couples with the engaged couple in a mentoring relationship.

dispensation
Special permission to depart from the usual requirements in a given circumstance.

natural family planning
A morally acceptable way to time pregnancies based on the observation of a woman's naturally occurring times of fertility and infertility.

mixed marriage
A marriage between a Catholic and a baptized non-Catholic.

disparity of cult
A marriage between a baptized Catholic and a nonbaptized person.

Whatever form this preparation takes, it includes information to help the couple better appreciate the Church's teaching on marriage. This information includes a focus on exploring the marriage promises that the couple will make and the skills necessary to live those promises. It also includes exploring a further understanding of marriage as an exclusive and faithful lifelong commitment that remains open to the possibility of children. This time of preparation also helps the couple to better understand themselves, especially the personal strengths and weaknesses they will bring into their marriage. Typically marriage preparation programs also focus on developing communication skills and providing basic information on **natural family planning** (see page 92 for additional information).

Most important, marriage preparation helps the engaged couple learn how to make their faith the foundation of their marriage. Couples learn (or refresh their memories) about the Church's teachings on marriage and the significance of the vows they are preparing to make to each other. They are also guided toward a fuller understanding of the importance of participating in the Church's prayer and sacramental life as a couple. Engaged couples are invited to reflect on the seriousness of their vocation to be spouses and possibly also parents and to prayerfully consider their new upcoming responsibility to live as witnesses of Christ's love for his Church.

Planning the Liturgy

While the couple goes through a marriage preparation program, they will also spend time planning the details of the wedding liturgy itself. However, because marriage is a public act that requires a liturgical celebration, the Church determines most of the words that will be spoken, including the wedding vows.

Still, the couple may be involved in many aspects of planning the liturgy. For example, they may select the readings, plan the music, and designate who will fill various roles at the Mass (i.e., lector, cantor, altar servers, and those who will bring up the gifts).

Catholic weddings—with very few exceptions—take place in Catholic churches. Unlike some non-Catholic Christian ecclesial communities, the Church typically does

Can Catholics Marry Non-Catholics?

The Church encourages Catholics to choose Catholic spouses. As Catholics we are called to make our faith the center of our lives; and if we are married, we are also called to share everything with our spouse. If spouses do not practice the same faith, then they cannot easily experience this very important area of life together. In addition, a household in which both parents actively practice their Catholic faith provides a strong environment for the spiritual formation of children in the Church.

That said, the Church does permit a Catholic to marry a non-Catholic. If a Catholic marries a baptized non-Catholic (such as a Baptist, Lutheran, or Episcopalian), the couple enters into what is called a **mixed marriage**. If a Catholic marries someone who is not Christian, this is called a marriage with **disparity of cult**.

The Church recognizes a marriage between a Catholic and another baptized Christian as both valid and sacramental. The marriage between a Catholic and a non-Christian is considered valid, but it is not considered sacramental. Only two baptized Christians can enter into a sacramental union.

To enter into a mixed marriage or an interfaith (or disparity of cult) marriage, a Catholic must first receive permission from the local diocesan bishop. Usually, the pastor of the Catholic spouse-to-be can help to obtain the appropriate permissions. The Catholic must promise that he or she will continue to practice the Catholic faith and will avoid any temptation that may lead to leaving the Catholic faith. The Catholic spouse must also do everything possible to ensure that any children resulting from the marriage will be baptized into and brought up in the Church. Further, the non-Catholic party must be made aware of these promises that the Catholic spouse-to-be is required to make.

Weddings between Catholics and non-Catholics typically take place apart from the celebration of a Mass, often in a Catholic church during a Liturgy of the Word. In some special situations, a Catholic can be allowed to marry a non-Catholic in a non-Catholic Christian wedding or in a religious ceremony of a different faith if he or she has a Catholic priest present as a witness. In interfaith or mixed marriages, the type of wedding is determined on a case-by-case basis according to personal and family circumstances.

© Bill Wittman/www.wpwittman.com

not allow wedding ceremonies to take place outside of the Church, such as at the beach, in a hotel ballroom, and so on. The Rite of Marriage is not just about the couple themselves; it is an event with significance for the whole Church. Being married in a church building is a sign that the couple will live out their vocation as members of the Body of Christ. ✝

Article 17 The Nuptial Mass

© MNStudio/Shutterstock.com

Marriage is a public vocation. Thus, the Sacrament of Matrimony is never private but always public, and always celebrated in church.

A wedding that takes place during a Eucharistic liturgy is called a nuptial Mass. Under ordinary circumstances, Catholics are encouraged to exchange wedding vows in the context of a Mass.

The entrance rite for a Catholic wedding typically begins with a procession. The liturgical ministers, followed by the priest, lead it. Although it is not absolutely forbidden, the Church does discourage the custom of the father of the bride "giving his daughter away," because the bride and bridegroom give *themselves* to each other in marriage as a union of equals.

After the entrance rite, the Liturgy of the Word proceeds as usual. Special readings are proclaimed from the Old and New Testaments and the Gospel, as is a Responsorial Psalm, that celebrate the vocation of marriage. Then the priest gives a homily on the spirituality of married love and the responsibilities that come with the Sacrament of Matrimony.

The Rite of Marriage

The Rite of Marriage itself takes place after the conclusion of the homily. During this ritual everyone present stands as a sign of respect for the dignity of the Sacrament. The priest briefly addresses the bride and bridegroom, reminding them of the seriousness of the step they are about to take. To ensure that both are free to marry, and that they fundamentally understand what their commitment to marriage will entail, the bride and bridegroom are each asked three questions.

The first question is, Have you come here freely and without reservation to give yourselves to each other in marriage? For the marriage to be valid, each partner must marry the other wholly out of his or her own free will. If either party feels coerced—either directly (such as being physically threatened) or indirectly (such as feeling pressured to marry)—then the Sacrament of Matrimony cannot be valid. Being free to marry also means that neither the bride nor the bridegroom has any legal impediments that would prevent a valid marriage.

As the first question indicates, the Sacrament of Matrimony requires both parties to commit without reservation. One cannot validly enter into a marriage if one has any intention of holding back or misrepresenting oneself. Marriage by its very nature requires a complete gift of one's

Who Is the Minister of the Sacrament of Matrimony?

In the Eastern Churches, the celebrating priest is the minister of the Sacrament of Matrimony. For the Sacrament to be valid, his blessing is required. It is through his clerical ministry that the bride and groom receive the sacramental graces of their vocation.

In the Latin Church, the priest or deacon is not the minister of the Sacrament of Matrimony, but a witness representing the Church. The actual ministers of the Sacrament are the bride and groom themselves. They confer the

Sacrament upon each other by declaring their mutual consent. Marriage is unique among the Seven Sacraments in that laypeople are its ordinary ministers.

But a valid sacramental marriage in the Latin Church still requires the involvement of clergy serving as a witness. A sacramental marriage can be witnessed by a deacon, priest, or bishop, although only a bishop or priest can celebrate a nuptial Mass.

© Bill Wittman/www.wpwittman.com

true self to one's husband or wife. Marrying without reservation also means that neither the bride nor bridegroom has serious doubts about the decision to marry. Grave doubts, reservations, and misrepresentation can make a marriage invalid because they impede the ability of each party to give full consent.

This first question therefore asks the couple to state their personal unreserved freedom in coming to the church for the Sacrament of Matrimony. In doing so, the bride and bridegroom give public testimony to the truth of their immanent marriage.

The second question asks, "Will you love and honor each other as man and wife for the rest of your lives?" (*Rite of Marriage*, 24). By responding in the affirmative, the bride and bridegroom demonstrate their intention to enter into a lifelong sacramental union and their understanding that marriage is a permanent state that is ended only by the death of one of the spouses.

The third and final question addresses the family that the couple will create: "Will you accept children lovingly from God, and bring them up according to the law of Christ and his Church?" (*Rite of Marriage*, 24). For their marriage to be valid, Catholic couples are required not only to be faithful to each other but also to allow their love to bear fruit in the form of children. This question can be omitted in situations in which there is no realistic possibility of the couple bearing children together, such as when the bride and bridegroom are advanced in years.

After the couple has publicly given their assent to these questions, thereby manifesting their intentions in seeking to marry, the priest invites them to declare their consent. The bride and bridegroom join their right hands, and they each individually pronounce the vow formula to each other. One possible vow formula is this: "I, N., take you, N., to be my wife [or husband]. I promise to be true to you in good times and in bad, in sickness and in health. I will love you and honor you all the days of my life" (*Rite of Marriage*, 25).

The celebrating priest witnesses and receives these vows in the name of the Church. After the vows are exchanged, the couple exchanges rings. The priest blesses the rings, and then each spouse places a ring on the other's finger with these words: "N., take this ring as a sign of my love and fidelity. In the name of the Father, and of the Son, and of the Holy Spirit" (*Rite of Marriage*, 28).

Finally, after the Lord's Prayer, the priest prays a special nuptial blessing over the newly married couple, asking that God's grace be poured down upon them as they begin their new life together. Afterward, the Mass continues as usual.

Weddings outside of Mass

Sometimes a Catholic Marriage may be celebrated outside of Mass. For example, in a marriage involving a non-Catholic, it could be that most of the family and friends of the non-Catholic spouse are also not Catholic and may have difficulty appreciating the full significance of a Eucharistic celebration. Or sometimes a wedding is celebrated by a deacon instead of a priest, perhaps because the bridal couple lives in a remote area where few priests are available to celebrate a Mass.

In such cases a Liturgy of the Word may be celebrated. A nuptial Liturgy of the Word includes some of the same biblical readings suggested for a nuptial Mass, followed by the Rite of Marriage itself. It concludes with general intercessions and a nuptial blessing.

Pray It!

The Nuptial Blessing

Here is an excerpt from the nuptial blessing that a priest or deacon prays over a newly married couple at their wedding:

> Father, keep them always true to your commandments.
> Keep them faithful in marriage
> and let them be living examples of Christian life.
>
> Give them the strength which comes from the gospel
> so that they may be witnesses of Christ to others.
> (Bless them with children
> and help them to be good parents.
> May they live to see their children's children.)
> And, after a happy old age,
> grant them the fullness of life with the saints
> in the kingdom of heaven.
>
> *(Rite of Marriage, 33)*

convalidation

A wedding ceremony in which a man and a woman in a civil marriage have their marital union recognized and blessed by the Church.

A celebration of the Sacrament of Marriage for a Catholic couple who has already entered a civil marriage usually also occurs outside of Mass. In a civil marriage, the secular government declares a couple legally married, and they are considered married for all legal purposes. But the Church does not consider such a marriage to be sacramentally valid, because a priest or deacon did not witness the marriage vows in a Catholic nuptial liturgy, which unites the couple in a sacramental union that no one can dissolve.

The Church considers it sinful for a couple to live together after exchanging only civil vows. However, there is a way for couples in a civil marriage to be reconciled with the Church. After receiving the Sacrament of Penance and Reconciliation, the couple can profess their marriage vows sacramentally in the presence of a priest or deacon in a simple ceremony called a **convalidation**. ✝

Part Review

1. How does the family of origin have the potential to influence one's future married life?

2. Why should a dating relationship be based on friendship?

3. Name two reasons why it is sinful to live together before marriage.

4. Describe the process of planning a Catholic wedding.

5. Is a Catholic allowed to marry a non-Catholic? If so, under what circumstances and conditions?

6. Why does the Church encourage engaged couples to celebrate their wedding during a Eucharistic celebration?

7. What questions does a priest or deacon ask a couple prior to witnessing their wedding vows? Why are these significant?

Part 3

Responsibilities of Those Who Are Married

Because Matrimony is a Sacrament at the Service of Communion and serves to build up families, society, and the Church, it is only natural that married couples take on certain responsibilities upon entering into the vocation of married life. Spouses have obligations toward each other, toward any children they have, and ultimately toward the Church.

Spouses are first called to live a life of deep and total communion with each other. In this way, they help each other to grow in faith, and they come to love God more deeply through their faithful love for each other.

If God blesses a husband and wife with children, then they have the responsibility of loving and caring for the gifts of life entrusted to them. Parents must care for not only the physical needs of their children but also their spiritual needs, guiding their children to a relationship with God.

Finally, a couple has a responsibility to live as witnesses to Christ's love for his Church. Spouses do so through their love and faithfulness toward each other and by their openness to new life.

The articles in this part address the following topics:

Article 18 A Call to Unity

The vocation of married life calls a man and a woman to live as one in a real sense. When a couple marries, the whole of their union becomes greater than the sum of its individual parts. In their unity a husband and wife can reflect God's love for his people in a clearer and more profound way than they could when they were single.

The Spirituality of Marriage

The whole spirituality of marriage is oriented toward God's love for his people and likewise Christ's love for his Church. Human marriage is ultimately a temporary earthly reality; we know that in Heaven we "neither marry nor are given in marriage" (see Matthew 22:30). Yet marital love can enable us to glimpse the love that reigns in Heaven. In this sense earthly marriage is like a school for understanding divine love.

Marriage teaches one how to love wholeheartedly. As an unmarried young person, you ideally have a lot of love in your life already. Like any real love, this love—for parents, siblings, friends, and other important people in your life—involves self-giving and concern for others. However, none of these loves is all-encompassing. You are not expected to love family and friends in a way that demands the absolute and irrevocable offering of your whole person.

This is not the case with marriage. Spouses are called to give themselves to each other wholly and without reserve. They share their hopes and dreams, successes and failures, and joys and sorrows. What deeply affects one spouse also affects the other. Married couples build their lives around each other. Spouses also give each other the gift of their physical person. Through the sexual intimacy proper to marriage, the spouses make a mutual and permanent offering of their very selves.

In the complete self-giving of a marriage, married couples learn how to love God with their whole selves. This love and the sacramental grace of marriage prepare them for eternal life in Heaven, where all will be called to love God with totality. In their married love, in which each spouse gives of himself or herself for the good of the other, spouses also gain

Theology of the Body

The title *Theology of the Body* refers to a series of talks given for Wednesday audiences by Pope Saint John Paul II between 1979 and 1984. In these talks the Pope articulated the Church's understanding of what it means for human beings to be created as embodied souls. The *Theology of the Body* comprehensively develops the Church's theological rationale for her teachings on issues such as chastity, marriage, procreation, and parenthood, as well as celibate consecrated life.

Although his *Theology of the Body* did not put forward any radically new thinking, Pope Saint John Paul II did present the Church's traditional teachings in a new way. Namely, he treated the Church's teachings on the human body as an important area of theology in its own right. In response, many Catholics have found that the *Theology of the Body* has helped them to better understand chastity as a goal to be embraced rather than simply as a list of restrictions.

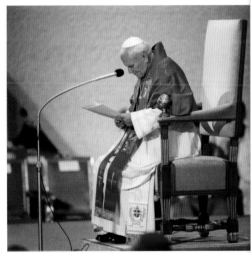

© LWA/Dann Tardif/Blend Images/Corbis

The *Theology of the Body* has also brought greater attention to what it means to be a human person viewed through the lens of faith. Not only did Pope Saint John Paul II present anew the Church's traditional understanding, but he also explored theological considerations of the human person by comparing and contrasting the Church's teachings with ideas from prominent secular philosophers.

Here are some of the basic principles of the *Theology of the Body*:

- God made each of us, male and female, in his own image.
- The basis for every human relationship is the love God has for each of us.
- Treat yourself and your body with respect, and expect the same from others.
- Dress modestly and not in a way that provokes inappropriate attention.
- God has given us the gift of sexuality. We should reserve this gift for the lifelong commitment of marriage and not diminish its dignity by engaging in illicit sexual activity.

a sense of how God loves us, his people. When a man and a woman marry, they make a commitment to remain faithful "in good times and in bad" (*Rite of Marriage*, 25). This means that even when a marriage goes through challenging times, when one spouse finds it difficult to feel loving toward the other, he or she is still called to love and remain committed to the marriage covenant. Witnessing how spouses grow in unconditional love shows all of us how God continues to love us, even when we stray from his commandments.

The grace of the Sacrament of Matrimony helps to bring the couple's love for each other to its fullness and strengthen their bond with each other.

© LWA/Dann Tardif/Blend Images/Corbis

A Call to Grow in Holiness

The experience of sharing one's life with another also helps husbands and wives to grow in holiness by providing ideal opportunities to develop virtue. The sacramental grace received in the Sacrament of Matrimony strengthens the spouses in their striving to grow closer to God and to reflect Christ's love to each other.

Married couples are called to consider each other's needs before their own and to be willing to make personal sacrifices for the good of the other. Because of our fallen human nature, this way of thinking does not always come easily to us; few of us are naturally inclined to give up our own way. Yet for married couples, the love they share makes this self-sacrifice possible. By learning to love each other completely, spouses learn to imitate Christ in his self-sacrificial love for us.

Pray It!

United in Love

The following is part of one of the readings that can be chosen for a Catholic wedding:

Love is patient, love is kind. It is not jealous, [love] is not pompous, it is not inflated, it is not rude, it does not seek its own interests, it is not quick-tempered, it does not brood over injury, it does not rejoice over wrongdoing but rejoices with the truth. It bears all things, believes all things, hopes all things, endures all things.

Love never fails. (1 Corinthians 13:4–8)

Praying with these Scripture verses can help us to grow in understanding of the kind of love that is at the heart of a healthy and holy marriage.

Daily life together also helps husbands and wives to grow in holiness. Along with the joys that come from the intimate friendship and loving support a married couple can share, living with another person also requires learning to accept his or her small faults, foibles, and idiosyncrasies. Shared daily life also requires learning to anticipate each other's needs and being ready to put them ahead of one's own at times. Over years of marriage, husbands and wives can help each other to grow in holiness and to become all-around better people. For example, they can teach each other to become more patient, trusting, generous, and humble. Just as a rock is ground and polished to reveal a gemstone, so also a healthy and loving marriage brings out the best in the spouses. In these and other ways, married couples are called to guide each other to a closer relationship with God. ✝

Article 19 A Call to Faithfulness

The Catholic view of marriage might seem strange to some people. Married couples promise to live their whole lives together, no matter how difficult things get. They also bind themselves to each other for life. To those who do not understand the beauty of the Church's teaching on marriage, this commitment might seem foolhardy—as though the spouses throw away all their personal freedom in one move.

We can learn much about the commitment of marriage from couples who have been married for many years.

But this mindset overlooks what anyone in a happy and loving marriage knows: true freedom is the freedom to bind yourself permanently to the one you love.

Lifelong Union

Marriage is one of the most solemn commitments that we can make and one of the most permanent bonds as well, enduring as long as both spouses are alive.

© Tyler Stalman/iStockphoto.com

This does not negate the existence of civil divorce. Typically marriage is recognized by the secular government, and government cannot comment on the specifically sacramental dimension of marriage, nor on marriage's spiritual significance, but can grant a civil divorce according to the secular legal system.

Yet even though the state permits civil divorce, this does not mean that divorce is a good or even generally acceptable reality. Many states allow couples to divorce on almost any grounds, even for frivolous reasons, and the divorce rate continues to grow. Sadly, this can encourage spouses simply to give up when the going gets tough, instead of remaining committed to working through the inevitable difficulties that come with marriage. Widespread divorce in turn undermines the stability and the importance of the family as the foundational unit of society.

The Church does acknowledge that physical separation of spouses is necessary, at least temporarily, in some unhealthy or dangerous circumstances. For example, if one spouse poses a serious threat to the health and safety of the other spouse or to the couple's children, then the Church permits and would even encourage the physical separation of the couple and their living apart. This separation may include civil divorce in some cases, but divorce must always be the exception, not the rule.

Civil divorce in and of itself is not a sin. It is possible to be a divorced Catholic in good standing, and the Church encourages those who are divorced to find spiritual support in the Sacraments of the Eucharist and Penance and Reconciliation. However, after a civil divorce, the spouses must receive an annulment from the Church before either can enter into a new civil marriage. Those who do enter into a new civil marriage without a declaration of nullity commit the sin of adultery and are a source of scandal for others. That does not mean they are separated from the Church. Indeed, as baptized persons, they should continue to participate in the life of the Church and the practice of their faith by bringing up their children in the Church and performing acts of charity and penance. Most important, they must continue to attend Sunday Mass to hear the Word of God. But as long as they continue to live in this situation, they are not eligible to receive the Sacraments except in danger of death. They are

Saints Thomas More and John Fisher and the Divorce of Henry VIII

The marriage bond is such a sacred commitment that some saints in the Church's history have chosen to die rather than to deny the permanence and exclusive nature of marriage. Two of these saints are Saint John Fisher and Saint Thomas More.

Saints John Fisher and Thomas More both lived in sixteenth-century England. The two were great friends, sharing a love of learning and scholarship and an even greater love of their Catholic faith. Saint John Fisher was a bishop, and Saint Thomas More was a married layman with four children. More was also a lawyer who served in the English government and eventually became chancellor of England, the second most powerful government position after the king himself.

Fisher and More were both close advisors of the reigning monarch, King Henry VIII. When Henry's first wife, Catherine of Aragon, was unable to bear a living male heir, Henry wished to divorce her in order to marry Anne Boleyn. When Pope Clement VII would not allow the king to divorce, Henry broke away from the Catholic Church and founded the Church of England, declaring himself its head.

The English bishops, except for Fisher, all followed Henry into the Church of England and subsequently approved his divorce. Likewise, More was one of the few men among the English nobility who refused to swear an oath supporting Henry's actions. Because of this, Saints John Fisher and Thomas More were charged with the crime of high treason and were convicted on perjured evidence. They were imprisoned in the Tower of London and executed within two weeks of each other. Saints John Fisher and Thomas More share a feast day on June 22.

Saint Thomas More

Saint John Fisher

annulment

The declaration by the Church that a marriage is null and void, that is, it never existed as a sacramental union. Catholics who divorce must have the marriage annulled by the Church to be free to marry once again in the Church.

also ineligible to serve as sponsors for those being baptized or confirmed.

Annulments

An **annulment** is distinct from a civil divorce in that it concerns the sacramental dimension of a marriage, and not the civil status of the marriage union. An annulment (formally called a "declaration of nullity") can be issued when the Church determines that there was a defect of consent, a defect of form, or the existence of an impediment to the marriage (see *Catechism*, 1625–1632). Other reasons for a declaration of nullity include one or both of the spouses lacking the psychological capacity to assume the essential obligations of marriage or if one or both spouses were forced into the marriage.

Before seeking an annulment in the United States, a couple must first obtain a civil divorce. Then either spouse can submit the case to a Church court, called a tribunal. The tribunal looks at all aspects of the spouses' courtship and marriage, including the statements of third-party witnesses confirming the spouses' accounts. Sometimes the tribunal will ask those involved in the annulment process to visit with a therapist to determine whether any serious emotional health issues could have affected the couple's freedom to marry or the ability to fully assume the essential obligations of marriage.

Live It!

Marriage Role Models

The world we live in doesn't always support committed marriage and family life. The media often presents images that devalue the marriage commitment. The reality of mobility and the loss of family ties, society's emphasis on personal freedoms, and the ease with which civil divorces are granted also contribute to the sense that marriage doesn't have to be a permanent commitment. Additional challenges to marriage and family life include financial burdens that cause a need for both parents to work outside the home and a general loss of the respect that is shown for the dignity of all human beings. Still many married couples and families continue to thrive and bear witness to the blessings the marital covenant brings to spouses and their children. Make it a goal to seek out married couples and families that might be examples to you as you learn more about this particular vocation.

Once all the evidence is gathered and considered carefully, the tribunal will make a determination regarding whether a declaration of nullity can be granted. When an annulment is granted, the former spouses are free to marry in the Church if they wish. ✝

Article 20 A Call to Fruitfulness

Husbands and wives are called to be not only faithful but also fruitful—that is, they are called to be open to the gift of children. One of the purposes for marriage is procreation. When a child is conceived through an act of marital intimacy, that child is a living manifestation of the parents' love for each other. In a special way, a child is a concrete sign of the powerful love that exists between two spouses. When we say that marital love must be fruitful, we mean that it should cooperate with God's love and be oriented to the new creation that a child represents.

The procreative aspect of marriage is also one reason why sexual intimacy is a sacred reality. God calls married men and women to participate as cocreators in the generation of new life. Every time a child is conceived, God creates and endows that child with an immortal soul. Because sexual relations can lead to the creation of a human being, one who is destined to live with God through all eternity, human sexuality should always be regarded with due reverence and respect for its awesome power.

Raising a Christian family is a unique and special way the laity participates in Christ's mission. What are some of the things your family has taught you about being Christian?

© fatihhoca/iStockphoto.com

Remaining Open to New Life

When married couples eliminate the possibility of pregnancy while having sexual intercourse, they reject their call to share in God's power to bring life into the world. The refusal of fertility has no place in God's plan for marriage because it turns the couple away from the greatest gift of marriage: children. Although the Church recognizes that couples should act responsibly in having children, the spacing of children should be accomplished through a method such as natural family planning (NFP), which emphasizes the union of the couple and their openness to life. All methods of **contraception**—including the use of chemicals; barrier

Natural Family Planning

The Church's prohibition of contraception does not mean that married couples are expected simply to have as many children as they are biologically able to have. Nor does it mean that couples need to actively and constantly try to become pregnant throughout their childbearing years.

Although contraception is immoral at all times and in all circumstances, the Church does recognize that there can be legitimate reasons for avoiding pregnancy or for seeking to space pregnancies in a certain way. For example, a couple may wisely seek to postpone pregnancy because of illness, a family crisis, or a time of economic difficulty. In these kinds of cases, natural family planning (NFP) provides a moral way to plan pregnancy.

NFP is based on the fact that a woman's body is more fertile at certain times in the menstrual cycle and naturally infertile at other times. NFP teaches married couples how to recognize the wife's fertile periods and to practice abstinence during those times to avoid pregnancy. NFP can also be used as an aid to achieve pregnancy, if the married couple observes fertile periods to know when they are more likely to conceive.

NFP is different from contraception because it respects God's design for the human body. Whereas contraception actively aims to destroy life-giving potential, NFP simply acknowledges that this life-giving potential is not always present. However, couples who use NFP are strongly encouraged to avoid developing a contraceptive mentality in which having children is seen as something to be avoided. They must never lose sight of the fact that children are always a blessing to be welcomed with love and trust in God's providence.

methods, such as condoms and diaphragms; and surgical sterilization—are morally wrong.

The gift of sexuality as expressed in marriage has a two-fold end: to deepen the joyful loving union of the spouses and to bring new life into the world. Both purposes are necessary and should not be separated, especially during the act of sexual intercourse. Doing so will have negative effects on the couple's relationship and their spiritual life. When practices that separate these purposes, such as artificial contraception, become widespread in society, it will have negative effects on the future of family life itself.

Contraception also encourages a mindset that sees children as problems to be avoided, rather than as precious gifts from God to be welcomed. Contraception can harden a couple's hearts, making them blind to the joy that comes from generously welcoming the new life that God wishes to entrust to them.

Taken to extremes, acceptance of contraception can also lead to a mentality that sees **abortion** as acceptable and to view children as an unwanted and problematic outcome of sexual intimacy. Abortion is the deliberate termination of a pregnancy by killing the unborn child. In the 1970s the United States made abortion legal, and many other countries have done the same. However, acts that are legal are not necessarily moral. Yet what is legal often becomes commonplace and can be mistakenly seen as morally acceptable. Today abortion has tragically become commonplace.

Abortion is a serious sin and is strongly forbidden by the Law of God. However, if the mother of the unborn child is critically ill and requires a medical procedure that indirectly results in the death of her unborn child, such a procedure is not an abortion and is recognized by the Church as necessary and morally acceptable. In such a case, the medical procedure is said to have a double effect: saving the life of the mother and ending the life of the child. The first is intended; the second is not. This tragic situation is morally tolerated because the death of the child is not directly intended.

Catholic Couples and Infertility

Many couples, far from seeking to prevent conception, deeply desire children but are infertile—that is, unable to

contraception
The deliberate attempt to interfere with the creation of new life as a result of sexual intercourse. It is morally wrong because a married couple must remain open to procreation whenever they engage in sexual intercourse.

abortion
The deliberate termination of a pregnancy by killing the unborn child. It is a grave sin and a crime against human life.

in vitro fertilization
The fertilization of a woman's ovum (egg) with a man's sperm outside her body. The fertilized egg is transferred to the woman's uterus. The Church considers the process to be a moral violation of the dignity of procreation.

conceive and give birth. Infertility can have a number of medical causes—sometimes known and sometimes not. Infertility can be a great cross for married couples to bear.

The Church supports the efforts of doctors and medical researchers to find cures for the underlying medical problems that cause infertility; however, many of today's widely used treatments for infertility are gravely immoral, because like contraception, they separate the unitive and procreative dimensions of sexual intimacy. Whereas contraception promotes the unitive aspect of sexuality at the expense of the procreative, artificial reproductive technologies attempt to create new life apart from sexual intimacy.

Children must be the outcome of the loving union of a husband and wife in sexual intercourse and not conceived through artificial means. Thus **in vitro fertilization**, which is creating a fertilized ovum in a laboratory and then implanting it in the woman's womb, is morally wrong. Artificial insemination, a fertility technique that artificially implants sperm in a woman's womb, is also morally wrong. The use of surrogate motherhood—placing a fertilized ovum in another woman's womb, letting the baby grow inside her, and after birth giving the newborn infant to the baby's biological mother and father—is also a serious moral offense.

The Church encourages couples who are unable to bear children to allow their love for each other to bear fruit through adoption or to express their generosity in other ways, such as working for and with people who are poor and vulnerable. ✝

Married couples can express God's love in a variety of ways.

© Ocean/Corbis

Article 21 Family Life

The vocation of married couples to whom God has given children goes well beyond welcoming new life. Parents are responsible for caring for, protecting, educating, and raising their children in faith and love. These may seem like daunting tasks, especially for new parents, but they are tasks that are supported by the sacramental grace that is received in the Sacrament of Matrimony.

Responsibilities toward Children

The most obvious duties of parents toward their children involve fulfilling their children's physical and emotional needs. Children have physical needs for food, clothing, shelter, medical care, and protection from dangerous situations. Children also have emotional needs that must be met, such as the need for human interaction, affection, and a feeling of basic security. Although theoretically any competent adult could provide such basic needs, parents are specially called by God to care for their own children.

The Rite of Baptism includes blessings for the child's parents that speak to the love and care they are to offer their children. Your parents may have heard the following or similar words when you were baptized: "May almighty God, who gives life on earth and in heaven, bless the parents of these children. They thank him now for the gift he has given them. May they always show that gratitude in action by loving and caring for their children" (*Rite of Baptism*, 70).

Catholic Wisdom

An Image of the Trinity

In the *Catechism of the Catholic Church*, we are reminded how families are the image of the Trinity:

The Christian family is a communion of persons, a sign and image of the communion of the Father and the Son in the Holy Spirit. In the procreation and education of children it reflects the Father's work of creation. It is called to partake of the prayer and sacrifice of Christ. Daily prayer and the reading of the Word of God strengthen it in charity. (2205)

Families are to be schools of virtue, teaching children God's Commandments, so that the children can live moral lives in accordance with God's Laws. Parents' efforts to nurture their children's faith are their way of living up to a call they received at their child's Baptism.

Parents' first and most important duty toward their children is to love them as unique individuals created in the image and likeness of God. They must bond with and care for their children as precious responsibilities entrusted to them. At the same time, parents also must recognize that their children are ultimately gifts on loan—they do not truly belong to the parents but to God.

Parents must respect the dignity of their children as human beings who are meant to have their own individual interior life with God and whom God will call to some particular vocation within the Church. Therefore parents must regard the vocational discernment of each child with appropriate reverence balanced with encouragement, guidance, and support.

Parents are also responsible for the education of their children. Because education helps to form children as people, it is a continuation of the parents' life-giving role. Parents' obligation to ensure the education of their children includes their children's academic and intellectual formation. Parents meet this obligation in part by sending their children to school (or by following a structured program of homeschooling).

Parenthood is both rewarding and challenging. Take some time to offer a prayer for all families that they may be strengthened and may continue to grow in love.

© Brooke Fasani Auchincloss/Corbis

Parents must remember, however, that they are their children's first educators, especially when it comes to their faith life. Parents do this first by creating a home in which love, respect, caring, forgiveness, service of others, and faith are the normal values practiced by everyone in the family. Beginning when the children are quite young, parents must teach them to have faith in God and to develop a relationship with God through prayer and the Sacraments. Parents are their children's first educators of faith, teaching them the truths revealed by God for our salvation.

The Family in the World Today

The particular cultural influences and social structures that families find themselves surrounded by have changed and continue to change in modern times. In his document *On the Role of the Christian Family in the Modern World (Familiaris Consortio)*, Pope Saint John Paul II points out the positive and negative aspects of the situation families find themselves in today:

> On the one hand, in fact, there is a more lively awareness of personal freedom and greater attention to the quality of interpersonal relationships in marriage, to promoting the dignity of women, to responsible procreation, to the education of children. . . . On the other hand, however, [there is] a mistaken theoretical and practical concept of the independence of the spouses in relation to each other; serious misconceptions regarding the relationship of authority between parents and children; the concrete difficulties that the family itself experiences in the transmission of values; the growing number of divorces; the scourge of abortion; the ever more frequent recourse to sterilization; the appearance of a truly contraceptive mentality. (6)

The entire Church is called to support families in the mission God has entrusted to them. Through prayer, appreciation, encouragement, and action toward creating a supportive environment, the Church demonstrates how important family life and the many gifts it has to offer are to the Church and to the world.

The Family as the Domestic Church

The family is often called the domestic Church. This is an affirmation that families should be a place where all the members can grow in their relationship with God, unite in prayer, and practice living the virtues. Parents should help their children to grow in their faith and in their relationship with God. Likewise, children should respect the authority of their parents.

The Holy Family—Jesus, Mary, and Joseph—is the perfect model of the family as the domestic Church. In one of his letters on the family, Pope Saint John Paul II wrote about how the Holy Family can help us to see the roles and responsibilities involved in family life:

> For every believer, and especially for Christian families, the humble dwelling place in Nazareth is an *authentic school of the Gospel.* Here we admire, put into practice, the divine place to make the family an *intimate community of life and love*; here we learn that every Christian family is called to be a small "*domestic Church*" that must shine with the Gospel virtues. Recollection and prayer, mutual understanding and respect, personal discipline and community asceticism (simple living) and a spirit of sacrifice, work and solidarity are typical features that make the family of Nazareth a model for every home.
> ("Angelus: Feast of the Holy Family," 2)

Family life should be marked by a communion of love. Although no family is perfect, family members are called to remember that they are not only natural brothers and sisters, or sons and daughters, to one another but also brothers, sisters, sons, and daughters in Christ. ✝

Why Isn't My Family Perfect?

Some families really struggle. Every family has ups and downs, but some families struggle with serious issues like divorce, alcoholism, mental illness, or physical and sexual abuse.

If you are living in a family that is struggling with problems like these, you probably want to cry out to God, "Why me?" And you should, because it isn't fair; it isn't the way God intends us to live. What can you do if you are in a family situation like this?

- **Find support.** See a counselor, join a support group, get active in your Church's youth group. Find a place where you can belong in healthy ways.
- **Talk to whomever in your family will listen.** If a problem is affecting you, it is also affecting other members of your family. You can work together to find little things to make your family better.
- **Pray.** Share your struggles with Jesus. He is with you and wants to share your burden. Pray for your family, that it can grow healthier. Pray for yourself, that you can find the strength you need.
- **Take action.** If someone is being hurt or neglected, don't accept it. Call the police or a social worker, or tell a teacher, a parish priest, a school counselor, or a youth leader. If that person can't provide all the help you need, ask him or her to direct you to another person or organization that can help. Sometimes it takes an intervention from the outside for a family to get healthy again.

Part Review

1. What responsibilities do married couples have toward each other? toward the children they may have? toward the wider Church community?

2. Briefly describe the spirituality of married life.

3. Describe the Church's teaching on the permanence of marriage, and explain how this teaching factors into the Church's practice regarding divorce and annulment.

4. What does it mean for a married couple to be open to new life? Why is this openness a serious obligation for all married couples?

5. What is NFP, and how is it different from contraception?

6. Name three responsibilities parents have toward their children. How do these relate to the idea of the family as the domestic Church?

Ordained Life

Part 1

Serving the Church through Ordained Ministry

Through the Sacrament of Holy Orders, a baptized man is given the grace to serve the Church as a deacon, priest, or bishop. As a distinct state of life, being ordained is a vocation centered on continuing the mission that Christ entrusted to his Apostles.

As one of the Seven Sacraments, Holy Orders was instituted by Christ himself at the Last Supper as a sign of his presence and priestly action in the Church. God willed that the saving ministry of Christ should continue on earth until the end of time. Although Christ ascended into Heaven, he did not abandon us. He ensured that his presence would remain with us through his Church and the Sacraments.

At the Last Supper, Christ called the twelve Apostles to continue his mission after his Ascension. He gave them the power and authority to administer the Sacraments in his name. Christ also entrusted the Apostles with the responsibility to care for his Church under the guidance of the Holy Spirit. In turn, the Apostles appointed other men to take their places after their deaths.

The articles in this part address the following topics:

Article 22 Christ, the High Priest

Thousands of years ago, many ancient polytheistic pagan religions incorporated a primitive idea of priesthood into their worship. Pagan priests were those who offered sacrifices—usually by ritually slaughtering livestock, such as sheep, cattle, lambs, or goats—to their gods in exchange for favors they sought, such as good weather, victory in war, or a bountiful harvest.

When the one, true God revealed himself to Abraham almost two thousand years before the birth of Christ, he showed humanity that he was a very different kind of God than the false gods the pagans worshipped. Unlike the pagan gods, the God of Israel was not a distant, limited entity who could be manipulated into acting a certain way through a ritual offering; rather, he was an all-powerful, ever-living, and all-loving being who desired a personal, loving relationship with the human beings he created. Sacrifices offered to the one, true God were to be expressions of adoration, gratitude, and communion.

The first priest mentioned in the Old Testament is Melchizedek (see Genesis 14:18). Melchizedek was a rather mysterious figure, identified only as "king of Salem" and a "priest of the most high God," who offered to God a sacrificial gift of bread and wine. Although little is known about Melchizedek, he is frequently mentioned in Scripture as a symbol for true priesthood.

Christ is the Head of the Church. He is the High Priest who has offered his life as a sacrifice, once and for all.

© Richard Paul Kane/Shutterstock.com

Later the Book of Exodus describes how Aaron, the brother of Moses, and the entire tribe of Levi were called by God to be priests for the nation of Israel. "You will be to me a kingdom of priests, a holy nation" (Exodus 19:6). Aaron and his successors' primary role was to preside over the Israelites' liturgical worship. This priesthood continued once the Israelites settled in the land God had promised them.

Around the year 960 BC, King Solomon, the son of the great King David, built a

spectacular temple for the worship of God. In the Temple, priests led the people in prayer and offered sacrifices. These sacrifices usually consisted of animal offerings or sometimes offerings of grain or oil. Often an animal, such as a lamb, was slain and offered to God as reparation for sin, either for the sin of an individual or for the collective sins of the whole community.

Because they were specially chosen by God and knew the one, true God, the whole nation of Israel was called to be a priestly people. It was only through the Israelites that God could be offered pleasing sacrifices. Yet at the same time, the Israelites who were specifically appointed priests were men called and consecrated to divine service. It was these priests who were "taken from among men and made their representative before God, to offer gifts and sacrifices for sins" (Hebrews 5:1).

This priesthood honored God with sacrifice and prayer and united the people in worship, but it could not bring salvation. Only the sacrifice of Christ would bring that about. The Church, however, sees in the priesthood of the Old Covenant a prefiguring of the ordained ministry that Jesus Christ himself established.

Foreshadowing Christ's Priesthood

Many events recorded in the Old Testament foreshadow the life of Christ, giving us a hint of what is to come. For example, Melchizedek's offering of bread and wine foreshadows the elements Christ used in offering us his own priestly sacrifice in the Eucharist (see Genesis 14:18–20). Abraham's willingness to sacrifice his son Isaac (see Genesis 22:1–13) reveals Christ's willingness to follow the Father's will even to the point of giving up his own life. And in the Book of Exodus, the Passover story helps us to understand how Christ's self-offering as the Lamb of God led us out of our slavery to sin.

Thus the rites of ordination for bishops, priests, and deacons include references to the priesthood of the Old Testament. At the ordination of bishops, reference is made to God's plan for salvation from the beginning:

> God the Father of our Lord Jesus Christ, . . .
> by your gracious word
> you have established the plan of your Church.
>
> From the beginning,
> you chose the descendants of Abraham to be your holy nation.
> You established rulers and priests,
> and did not leave your sanctuary without ministers to serve
> you. . . .[1]
>
> (Catechism of the Catholic Church [CCC], 1541)

When priests are ordained, the liturgy references the seventy wise men Moses chose to help him govern God's people and reminds us of the first high priest, Aaron. Addressing God the Father, the bishop who is ordaining the priests prays:

> you extended the spirit of Moses to seventy wise men. . . .
> You shared among the sons of Aaron
> the fullness of their father's power.[2]
>
> (CCC, 1542)

At the ordination of deacons, the sons of Levi are referenced:

> You established a threefold ministry of worship and service,
> for the glory of your name.
> As ministers of your tabernacle you chose the sons of Levi
> and gave them your blessing as their everlasting inheritance.[3]
>
> (CCC, 1543)

Catholic Wisdom

In What Sense Is Jesus a Priest?

The following quotation from Pope Benedict XVI from a homily for the Feast of Corpus Christi addresses the priesthood of Christ, which is shown through his unique sacrifice on the Cross:

> [Jesus] became the High Priest for having taken on himself all the sin of the world, as "Lamb of God." It is the Father who confers this priesthood on him at the very moment in which Jesus goes through the passage from his death to his Resurrection. ("Homily of His Holiness Benedict XVI," 2010)

atonement

Reparation for
wrongdoing or sin and
reconciliation with
God, accomplished for
humankind by Christ's
sacrifice.

As Abraham is our "father in faith" ("Eucharistic Prayer I"), our bishops, priests, and deacons inherit the spiritual blessings given to the sons of Aaron and Levi.

The Priesthood of Christ

Jesus Christ is the summit and perfect fulfillment of this Old Testament priesthood. He is the unique "high priest according to the order of Melchizedek" (Hebrews 5:10). Christ is the ultimate High Priest, with a "priesthood that does not pass away" (7:24).

In his suffering and death on the Cross, Christ offered his very self in **atonement** for the sins of humanity. He was both the sacrificial Lamb of God as well as the priest who offered the sacrifice.

Christ instituted the Eucharist as a memorial of his death and Resurrection. This action, a pledge of love offered to his disciples, enabled them to share in the Paschal Mystery, to be nourished by the gift of himself and thus enter into a true communion with him. Christ's sacrifice of the Cross, the priestly self-offering of himself, is made present at every Mass, where the bishop or priest acts *in persona Christi capitis,* "in the person of Christ the Head." Therefore the Eucharist is an everlasting memorial to God's saving love for us. ✝

Article 23 Continuing Christ's Saving Mission

The priestly mission of Jesus Christ was that of reconciling God and humanity. He accomplished this through his sacrifice on the Cross. And because Christ is the fullness of Revelation, through him we come to know God in a new and deeper way. By his coming to earth as man while remaining God, Christ made it possible for us to attain union with God.

During his time on earth, Christ made God's redemptive love present to us in a special way through his words and deeds. His teachings, miracles, prayers, love for all people, care and attention to those who were poor and outcast, and his saving death on the Cross were all revelations of God's tremendous love for us.

Forty days after his Resurrection from the dead, Jesus Christ ascended into Heaven. Yet he did not abandon his disciples on earth. He promised to remain with us forever and sent the Holy Spirit to guide us. But Christ also willed that his saving works should continue until the end of time. To do this he established the Seven Sacraments, which are "actions of the Holy Spirit at work in his Body, the Church" (*CCC*, 1116). And in order that the Sacraments would be administered in his name and in his person, Christ instituted the holy priesthood among his disciples.

The Calling of the Twelve

In his earthly ministry, Christ had a great variety of disciples from all walks of life. However, he also chose some of his followers to be a part of an especially close circle. We call these twelve men the Apostles.

Jesus spent a great deal of time forming the Apostles in their faith and knowledge of God. Many of Jesus' words recorded in the Gospels are taken from conversations he had with them.

Mosaic of Peter receiving the keys to the Kingdom (see Matthew 16:13–20).

© Jule_Berlin/Shutterstock.com

Jesus invested so much time and energy into the formation of the twelve Apostles because they were the ones whom he had chosen to continue his ministry after his return to the Father. The Apostles were to spread the Good News of salvation and administer the Sacraments in Christ's name. At the Last Supper, Jesus instituted the Eucharist and commissioned the Apostles to continue offering the Eucharistic sacrifice until the end of time.

Pentecost

Though the twelve Apostles had an extraordinary vocation, in many other respects they were very ordinary men. Most of them led unremarkable lives before they met Jesus. For example, Saints James and John were fishermen. Once they heard the call of Jesus, they dropped their fishing gear right where it was in order to follow him (see Matthew 4:21–22).

Saint Peter was a fisherman too. Upon hearing Christ's call, he at first protested, saying that he was too sinful for such a profound calling (see Luke 5:8).

It took the Apostles some time before they really understood the mission to which they were called. Many of them at first thought that Jesus intended to use his divine power to found an earthly kingdom. Because of their incomplete understanding, they were especially distressed and confused by the events of Jesus' Passion, death, and Resurrection.

Even in his post-Resurrection time on earth, Christ continued to guide his Apostles to a fuller understanding of the truth. Yet at Jesus' Ascension into Heaven, the Apostles were still unsure of exactly what Christ had called them to do (see Acts of the Apostles 1:10–11). But nine days later, as they were gathered together in prayer, the Holy Spirit came down among them (see 2:1–13). They received the Gifts of the Holy

The Successor to Saint Peter

Do you ever wonder why we have a Pope in charge of the worldwide Church? The Pope is the head of the Church on earth because he is the direct successor to Saint Peter.

We know from Scripture that Christ called Saint Peter to be the head of the Apostles. "And so I say to you, you are Peter, and upon this rock I will

build my church" (Matthew 16:18). Because Saint Peter died while he was serving as Bishop of Rome, all future Bishops of Rome are considered to be standing in the place of Saint Peter.

The Bishop of Rome has been considered the first among bishops in his authority since the very beginning of the Church. After the death of Saint Peter, the Bishop of Rome was consulted as the highest authority in the Church, even at a time when some of the other original twelve Apostles were still alive.

Spirit and came to understand God's plan for the continuing work of salvation as well as their own role within this plan.

After Pentecost the Apostles went to every place in the known world, preaching the Gospel and administering the Sacraments in Christ's name. They founded Christian communities in the cities where they traveled, providing inspired guidance and leadership to the first "dioceses."

successors
A successor is a person who succeeds, or comes after, another as office holder. Bishops, led by the Pope, the Bishop of Rome, are the successors of the Apostles.

The Apostles Choose Successors

Jesus commissioned the Apostles to continue his work on earth, guided by the Holy Spirit, until the end of the world. However, the individual Apostles were still mortal men and they knew that they would need to appoint **successors** to continue this mission. Because they had been entrusted with Christ's own authority, and guided by the Holy Spirit, they were able to call other men to share in the priesthood of Christ just as they themselves had been called to this mission. We see evidence of this in Scripture. To fill the place of Judas Iscariot, the Apostle who had hanged himself following his betrayal of Jesus, the eleven remaining Apostles chose Matthias and incorporated him into their ministry (see Acts of the Apostles 1:26).

Eventually, all the Apostles would be succeeded in ministry by others. Through the centuries the successors of the Apostles would continue to appoint successors. This is why, millennia after the Ascension of Christ, we still have men who are truly called to share in Christ's priesthood as bishops. ✝

Pray It!

Apostolic Succession and the Prayers of Ordination

In the prayer of consecration for the ordination of bishops, we can see clearly the connection with the original twelve Apostles:

> Pour out now upon these chosen ones that power which is from you, the Spirit of governance whom you gave to your beloved Son, Jesus Christ, the Spirit whom he bestowed upon the holy Apostles, who established the Church in each place as your sanctuary for the glory and unceasing praise of your name. (*Rite of Ordination*, 83)

Make sure to include the bishops and all those in leadership roles within the Church in your daily prayers.

Article 24 A Threefold Ministry

The mission that Christ entrusted to his Apostles, which they would later confer upon the bishops who would come to serve in their place, is threefold: to teach, to govern, and to sanctify. Let's take a look at each of these aspects of a bishop's ministry.

To Teach

Before he ascended into Heaven, Christ commissioned the Apostles to "make disciples of all nations, . . . teaching them to observe all that I have commanded you" (Matthew 28:19–20). Therefore the Apostles and all their successors are obligated to be teachers of the faith.

One facet of this mission is the call to spread the Good News as widely as possible. The Apostles branched out to every part of the world accessible to them at their time in history. For example, pious traditions hold that from Jerusalem, Saint John journeyed to what is now Turkey, and that the Apostle Thomas died preaching the Gospel in India.

In the early days of the Church's history, evangelization was a dangerous undertaking. Often the bishops, priests, and deacons of the early Church preached the Gospel not only with their words but also with the witness of their lives, dying as martyrs under the Roman emperors. After Christianity became an accepted religion within the Roman Empire

Live It!

Thinking with the Church

Because the Magisterium teaches the truth with authority, does this mean that the Church does not want us to think for ourselves?

The short answer is no. The Church has always encouraged her members to be critical thinkers. Many saints throughout history have asked challenging questions about the faith. Often it is only when individuals ask these tough questions that we can come to a deeper knowledge of the truth.

If you have trouble understanding why the Church teaches certain things, it is okay to ask searching questions. But at the same time, it is crucial to explore fully what the Church says in those matters. It is possible to ask hard questions about faith with an attitude of trust, love, and respect for the Church, trusting that the Holy Spirit will guide you.

in the fourth century, missionaries such as Saint Patrick and Saint Boniface brought the Good News to the pagan tribes of northern Europe. Later missionaries, such as Saint Francis Xavier and Saint Isaac Jogues, introduced Christianity to the peoples of East Asia and North America.

Today bishops (and by extension priests and sometimes deacons) teach by preaching the Gospel and explaining Scripture in their homilies, by explaining the Church's teachings to individuals, by guiding converts to the faith, and by the example of their lives.

Along with working to spread the faith, the clergy also have the responsibility to ensure that Christians are able to receive the Church's teachings without error. Although God revealed himself to us most fully in the person of Christ, it is still possible for us as fallible human beings to make mistakes in our understanding of who God is.

But because God wants us to understand the truth, he gives the Church the special gift of his divine guidance. In matters pertaining to faith (what we believe about God) and morals (how we are to live our lives), God protects the Church from ever falling into error.

Bishops are called to manifest this gift of being guided by the Holy Spirit and they are likewise charged with the responsibility of protecting the treasure of the Church's true teachings. Ordained bishops act as part of the **Magisterium**, the official teaching office of the Church, when they carry out their mission of teaching the truths of the faith with authority in communion with the Pope and with their brother bishops throughout the world.

Magisterium
The Church's living teaching office, which consists of all bishops, in communion with the Pope, the Bishop of Rome.

Within his diocese, a bishop is the visible source and foundation of unity. He is a living symbol that his particular church is unified with the universal Church. Who is your local bishop(s)?

To Govern

Ultimately, Christ is the head of his Church, and God guides and protects the people who are his own. Yet Christ still willed for his Church to be an institution of human beings.

Any association of human beings needs some form of leadership. Jesus Christ is the head, and therefore the ultimate leader, of the Church, but he still calls the ordained as his representatives for the fruitful governance of the Church on earth.

The bishops, together with their assisting clergy, are called in many concrete ways to govern the Church as Christ's instrument and representative. For example, they need to ensure that the Church is using its material resources wisely, both on the diocesan and parish levels. The bishops also need to oversee and organize Catholic institutions, such as universities and charitable organizations, to be sure that the faith is being presented and represented correctly. Bishops are also responsible for the well-being of the consecrated persons in their dioceses and can establish new religious communities if they discern that this is the will of God. Within certain limits each bishop can also set policies regarding the liturgical and sacramental practices within his diocesan territory.

To Sanctify

The word *sanctify* means "to make holy." The way that bishops and priests assist their people in becoming holy is through the celebration of the Sacraments. In their administration of the Sacraments, bishops, together with their priests, act in the person of Christ to sanctify their people.

© Bill Wittman/www.wpwittman.com

Although it is God alone who can truly sanctify in the proper sense of the word, bishops and priests are called to be Christ's instruments in the sanctification of the faithful by providing them with the Sacraments. For example, in the Sacrament of Baptism, the clergy work with God to restore their people to the life of grace, which allows the people to be

What Is Canon Law?

Although bishops are empowered to set policies for their local dioceses in certain areas, and even priests who serve as pastors can make decisions regarding the best way to administer their parish, many ecclesiastical rules are binding for all Roman Catholics everywhere. These rules are gathered together in a single book called the *Code of Canon Law*. (The Eastern Churches have their own similar, but separate, system of Canon Law.)

The *Code of Canon Law* contains almost two thousand individual rules, called canons, which cover various issues, such as who can administer or receive which Sacraments and under what circumstances; how Church organizations are to buy or sell property; the responsibilities of bishops, priests, and deacons; rules for the administration of Catholic schools; how religious communities are to be founded and organized; and how violations to the code itself are to be handled.

Many canons in the *Code of Canon Law* reflect divinely inspired truth. However, unlike Sacred Scripture, the *Code of Canon Law* itself is not a divinely inspired text. The Church can modify Canon Law whenever she discerns that a clarification is needed. At all times, however, the entire *Code of Canon Law* naturally finds its basis in the Church's teachings of faith and morals.

It may seem burdensome to the faithful for the Church to have so many rules. But in fact Canon Law exists to make sure that all the members of the Church are treated fairly and in accord with their dignity as adopted sons and daughters of God. The very last canon in the *Code of Canon Law* famously expresses the reason for the existence of Canon Law in the first place: "The salvation of souls, which must always be the supreme law in the Church, is to be kept before one's eyes" (1752).

made holy through communion with God. In the Sacrament of Penance and Reconciliation, the clergy help those who have sinned to return to a state of grace by reconciling them with God and with the Church. The grace of the Sacrament of Penance also helps the faithful to remain holy in the face of future temptation.

Priests and bishops also provide for the sanctification of their people through their offering of the Holy Sacrifice of the Mass, in which they act as Christ's representatives on earth. The Mass enables the faithful to receive the Eucharist, which brings them to an especially close union with Christ. In the Mass priests also present their peoples' offerings to

God so that these offerings may be sanctified. This is true in the sense of the offering of the bread and wine at Mass. But in their participation at Mass, the faithful are also presented with an opportunity to offer a gift of themselves to God. ✝

Part Review

1. What do we mean when we speak of Christ as the High Priest?

2. Describe how the Old Testament concept of priesthood relates to the priesthood of Christ.

3. What was Christ's purpose in calling the twelve Apostles?

4. How is the calling of the Apostles still relevant to the Church today?

5. What do we mean when we say that the bishops are called to teach, govern, and sanctify?

6. What is the function of the Magisterium?

Part 2

The Three Degrees of Holy Orders

The Sacrament of Holy Orders includes three degrees: bishop, priest, and deacon. Each has a different role within the Church.

A bishop receives the fullness of the Sacrament of Holy Orders and can administer all the Sacraments. He is empowered to sanctify the Church through his ministry of the Sacraments and the Word, to govern the Church in the spirit of service, and to protect the truth of the Church's teachings.

A priest is the bishop's coworker. He assists the bishop in continuing the ministry of the Apostles. A priest ministers to a specific parish (or parishes) in a diocese, preaches the Gospel, offers the Holy Sacrifice of the Mass, and administers the Sacraments.

Deacons are also called to service in the Church, but their ministry differs from that of priests. They serve by assisting with the celebration of the Eucharist, including reading the Gospel and giving the homily, as well as through charitable service to those who are poor and in need.

The articles in this part address the following topics:

Article 25 Bishops

In his Letter to the Ephesians, Saint Paul writes that Christ calls "some as apostles, others as prophets, others as evangelists, others as pastors and teachers, to equip the holy ones for the work of ministry, for building up the body of Christ" (4:11–12).

Saint Paul implies that all these callings are necessary for the proper functioning of the Church. Despite the fact that this letter was written nearly two thousand years ago, it is easy for us to see how many of these offices play a role in the Church today. We are familiar with pastors and teachers and those who evangelize by spreading the Good News. We may even know some people who could be considered "modern-day prophets." But what about Saint Paul's mention of apostles? We know that our Church was built on the foundation of the Twelve whom Jesus called, but is there some way we continue to have apostles in the Church today?

The Greek word *apostolos* literally means "one who is sent." We say the Church is apostolic because she is founded on Jesus' Apostles.

© Zvonimir Atletic/Shutterstock.com

Live It!

Understanding the Different Titles of Bishops

Most bishops are assigned to be the chief shepherd and primary administrator of a diocese. Bishops exercise this ministry under different titles: A *diocesan bishop* is the chief shepherd of a diocese. An *auxiliary bishop* is a bishop who assists a diocesan bishop in his responsibilities. An *archbishop* is the chief shepherd of an archdiocese, who also bears indirect responsibility for one or more neighboring dioceses within his metropolitan (or provincial) territory. A *cardinal* is a member of the college responsible for electing new popes. Many cardinals are also bishops or archbishops.

Can you name the bishop of your diocese? Take time to learn who your bishop is and to learn a little bit about him.

The Apostles' Successors

Though the vocation of the first Apostles as pastors and leaders of the early Church is certainly unique, apostleship has been a fundamentally important ministry in the Church throughout history and up to the present. The vocation of apostle today is fulfilled in the ministry of our bishops.

Each bishop ordained is in the line of **Apostolic Succession** that extends back to the twelve Apostles and thus to Christ himself. This gives each bishop a place of chief dignity in the Church. Together all the bishops of the world form what is called the **college of bishops**, which receives its authority from its union with the Pope, the successor of Saint Peter and the head of the college.

Bishops are able to serve as successors to the Apostles because they have received the fullness of the Sacrament of Holy Orders. Bishops receive a special outpouring of the Holy Spirit at their ordination. Deacons and priests receive the Sacrament of Holy Orders, but only bishops receive the fullness of the Sacrament.

Bishops are able to administer all seven Sacraments. At their ordination to the **episcopate**, bishops become empowered to confer the three degrees of the Sacrament of Holy Orders. Because this Sacrament is the Sacrament of the apostolic ministry, only bishops, the Apostles' successors, can confer it.

Caring for a Diocese

New bishops are chosen from among the ranks of faithful priests. Only the Pope can call a man to become a bishop. Usually a new bishop is asked by the Pope to lead the people of a particular Church, or a **diocese.**

The bishop is the primary person responsible for teaching, governing, and sanctifying the people in the diocese entrusted to his care. The vocation of a bishop is to act as a shepherd, guiding and protecting the members of his flock. He is also called to act as a spiritual father for the people in his diocese.

Because a bishop is a member of the college of bishops, his concern is not for his own diocese alone. He has the responsibility of working for the good of the universal

Apostolic Succession
The uninterrupted passing on of apostolic preaching and authority from the Apostles directly to all bishops. It is accomplished through the laying on of hands when a bishop is ordained in the Sacrament of Holy Orders as instituted by Christ. The office of bishop is permanent, because at ordination a bishop is marked with an indelible, sacred character.

college of bishops
The assembly of bishops, headed by the Pope, that holds the teaching authority and responsibility in the Church.

episcopate
The position or office of a bishop.

diocese
Also known as a "particular" or "local" Church, the regional community of believers, who commonly gather in parishes, under the leadership of a bishop. At times a diocese is determined not on the basis of geography but on the basis of language or rite.

Who Is the Ordinary Minister of Confirmation?

Confirmation is the Sacrament in which the Gifts of the Holy Spirit are strengthened within us. In the Latin Church—to which most Catholics in the West, including the United States, belong—bishops are the ordinary ministers of Confirmation.

In the Latin Church, a priest has the power to administer Confirmation in some circumstances, such as when he receives new converts to the faith at the Easter Vigil or if an unconfirmed member of the faithful is in danger of death. But in the Eastern Churches, the priest is the ordinary minister of Confirmation, and the standard tradition in these churches is for infants to be confirmed immediately after their Baptism.

Why is there this difference between Eastern Catholics and Western, or Latin, Catholics? In the early Church, the practice was for new Christians to receive all three Sacraments of Christian Initiation together in one liturgy with the local bishop presiding. But when the number of converts continued to increase, it became impossible for the bishop to attend every Baptism. Two different practices emerged as a result.

In the Latin Church, the bishop continued to confirm the baptized. The focus was on the twelve Apostles who stood in the place of Christ. To help the community keep in mind the strong connection between the local bishop and the ministry of Jesus, the Latin Church delayed Confirmation until a point in time when the bishop himself could administer the anointing.

The Eastern Churches kept the celebrations of Baptism and Confirmation together to emphasize the unity of the Sacraments of Christian Initiation. For Eastern Catholics, their connection with the bishop did not necessarily demand the bishop's physical presence, as this connection was already made clear in the oil consecrated by the bishop. Thus the Sacrament of Confirmation could be administered by a priest on an ordinary basis, allowing for Baptism and Confirmation to be celebrated regularly in the same liturgy.

Church, in communion with the Pope, the Bishop of Rome and the successor to Saint Peter.

On a practical level, a bishop's ministry includes many responsibilities. For example, a bishop must oversee the function of all parishes, schools, and charitable outreach programs in his diocese. This typically involves personal visits along with other forms of correspondence. A bishop promotes and discerns vocations to the priesthood within his diocese, and he has the responsibility of placing individual priests on assignment where they can do the most good for the Church. A bishop also writes and preaches to the people of his diocese. Most bishops publish periodic pastoral letters addressing what they see as their diocese's most pressing spiritual needs.

The celebration of the Eucharist is a central aspect of a bishop's sacramental ministry. A bishop regularly offers Mass at his diocese's cathedral and may also celebrate Mass at the parishes, schools, or other diocesan institutions he visits. A bishop also fulfills sacramental roles that only a bishop can fulfill. For instance, only a bishop can ordain new priests for his diocese. A bishop is also responsible for consecrating the holy oils that will be used in the administration of the Sacraments throughout his diocese at the Chrism Mass during Holy Week. He is also the minister of Confirmation in the Latin Church. (In the Eastern Churches, the priest is the ordinary minister of Confirmation, also called "Chrismation.")

A bishop's vocation is symbolized by many signs and symbols. For example, you may have noticed that a bishop wears a ring and sometimes wears a miter and carries a crozier. The ring is a sign of the bishop's fidelity to the Church. It reminds him that he is "married" to the Church and to his specific diocese, meaning that he will give the Church the first place in his life and that he will love the Church and her people with the same strength of love as he would have given to a wife and children. The miter, a unique, pointed hat that a bishop wears during liturgical ceremonies, is a symbol of the bishop's governing authority. A crozier is a ceremonial shepherd's staff, which represents the bishop's call to care for Christ's flock. ☩

© Bill Wittman/www.wpwittman.com

Article 26 Priests

presbyterate
The name given to priests as a group, especially in a diocese; based on the Greek word *presbyter*, which means "elder."

Priests are ordained men who have received the ministerial priesthood through their reception of the Sacrament of Holy Orders. They are called, ordained, and sent to preach the Word of God and to administer the Sacraments to the faithful. This role developed as the early Church grew, and the Apostles and their successors ordained priests to become their coworkers. Priests are ordained today to serve in this same role, becoming coworkers of the bishop and assisting him in the fulfillment of the mission Jesus Christ entrusted to the Apostles. Together with their bishop, priests form the **presbyterate**. Through their bond with their bishop, priests share in the apostolic ministry of teaching, sanctifying, and governing.

© Bill Wittman/www.wpwittman.com

The priests of a diocese help and advise the local bishop. With the bishop, each priest is responsible for a particular church.

One way priests participate in the bishop's ministry of teaching is through the preaching of the Gospel, especially in the homily at Mass. They fulfill the mission of sanctification through the celebration of the sacred liturgy, especially the Sacraments, which make people holy in a real way. Priests also share the bishop's task of governing (ruling and shepherding God's people) in part through administrative responsibilities, such as serving as a pastor of a parish, but also through the moral guidance they provide for the faithful in their care.

Diocesan Priests and Religious Order Priests

For men called to the priesthood, there are two distinct paths to follow: the diocesan priesthood or priesthood as part of a religious community. The two paths share common characteristics, but there are also some important differences between them.

Why Do We Call Priests "Father"?

Catholics usually refer to priests as Father. This is a term of respect that expresses the relationship the faithful are to have with their priests. Priests are called to be spiritual fathers. Just as natural fathers provide for their families' material and emotional needs, the priest is a spiritual father who provides for the spiritual needs of the souls entrusted to his care.

Sacred Scripture is clear that Father is an appropriate designation for spiritual leaders. Saint Stephen, under the inspiration of the Holy Spirit, addresses the Jewish leaders as fathers in the Book of Acts of the Apostles (see 7:2). In the First Letter to the Corinthians, Saint Paul addresses his converts as his "beloved children" (see 4:14), and tells them that he became their father in Christ through the Gospel. He goes on to say, "Therefore, I urge you, be imitators of me" (4:16). Like a father educates his children through his words and example, Saint Paul teaches his disciples by his word as well as his life.

© Bill Wittman/www.wpwittman.com

Diocesan Priests

A diocesan priest is a priest who is a part of a particular Church, or diocese. He engages in his priestly ministry under the direction of his diocesan bishop, and his priestly ministry is usually spent in the service of the faithful within the diocese's geographic territory. A diocesan priest is officially **incardinated** into his diocese—that is, he first officially "belongs" to a particular local church and its people—when he is ordained a deacon. Becoming a deacon is part of the process of becoming a priest, which we will explore shortly.

incardinated
Placed under the authority of a particular bishop or the superior of a religious community.

Liturgy of the Hours

Also known as the Divine Office, the official, public, daily prayer of the Catholic Church. The Divine Office provides standard prayers, Scripture readings, and reflections at regular hours throughout the day.

Diocesan priests make promises to obey their bishop, to pray the **Liturgy of the Hours**, and to remain faithful in their commitment to chaste celibacy. Many diocesan priests live a simple lifestyle for the sake of bearing a Christian witness, for solidarity with the poor, and as an imitation of Christ. However, diocesan priests do not make vows of poverty, so they are allowed to earn money for themselves and to own personal property.

Religious Order Priests

A religious order priest belongs to a particular religious order, such as the Dominicans, Franciscans, or the Society of Jesus (the Jesuits). In many religious orders, priests are ordained only after they have made their final commitment to the religious community. Most often this final commitment takes the form of making formal vows of poverty, chastity, and obedience. However, in some orders, such as the Society of Jesus, priests are ordained before they profess their final vows.

A man is ordained a religious priest by a bishop at the request and with the permission of that man's particular religious superior (the leader of his religious community). Although all priests are required to respect their bishop, after ordination a religious priest is obedient to the superior of his religious community rather than to the local bishop directly. Because a religious priest is also vowed to poverty, any money or property he might receive belongs not to him but to his community.

Because religious orders are typically founded for the sake of meeting some special need within the Church, most religious order priests live out their priesthood while

Pray It!

"And with Your Spirit"

At Mass when the priest says, "The Lord be with you," the people respond by saying, "And with your spirit." In this phrase the word *spirit* refers to the gift of the spirit a priest receives from God at his ordination. The people are offering their prayer that God will provide his assistance and guide the priest to fulfill the gift of the spirit given to him at ordination. Be attentive to these words the next time you say them at Mass, and ask for God's guidance for the priest presiding at Mass and for all priests.

engaging in the particular mission for which their order was founded. For example, many Jesuit priests teach in high schools and colleges because their order, the Society of Jesus, was founded in part for the sake of evangelizing through education. Franciscan priests, on the other hand, often work directly with those who are poor, as this was part of the focus of their founder, Saint Francis.

The Ministry of a Priest

The ministry of a priest, like the priesthood itself, is rooted firmly in Jesus Christ. A priest's identification with Christ finds its fullest expression in the preaching of the Gospel and the administration of the Sacraments.

Priests are ministers of the Sacrament of the Eucharist and preside over Eucharistic celebrations. They have the authority from Christ to absolve sins through the Sacrament of Penance and Reconciliation. They grant forgiveness and healing to the suffering through the Sacrament of Anointing of the Sick, and they stand in the place of Christ when they witness and bless the exchange of vows between a man and a woman in the Sacrament of Matrimony. Priests are also the ministers of the Sacrament of Baptism, through which we are forgiven of Original Sin and welcomed into the Body of Christ, the Church.

Priests minister wherever their bishop or religious superior sends them. Because the Church has a wide variety of spiritual needs, a priest could be assigned to a number of different ministries over the course of his priestly life. For example, a priest might teach in a school, work in the central diocesan office, serve on a marriage tribunal, minister to the sick as a hospital chaplain, or form future priests as a seminary professor or vocation director.

Most diocesan priests and some religious priests are assigned to minister in parishes. A parish priest may serve as a pastor, or head, of a parish or as one of several priests in any number of supportive roles to the pastor. Regardless of his specific role in the parish, the mission of a parish priest is to make Christ present to people from all walks of life, at every point in their lives.

By receiving the Sacrament of Holy Orders, a priest is configured to Christ in a particular, radical way, standing in the place of Christ as the head of his Body, the Church, and representing Christ to the community of believers. Through the ministry of priests, the Lord's grace is poured out upon the faithful, and the people are able to encounter God in a real way. ✝

Article 27 Deacons

After Pentecost the Apostles found themselves in the middle of a dilemma. The early Church had quickly begun to organize itself into a structured community, complete with the charitable outreach of supporting widows and the poor. In the midst of this outreach, however, the early Christians began to complain about the efficacy of these works of mercy because it appeared as though some people were receiving more help than others. "At that time, as the number of disciples continued to grow, the Hellenists complained against the Hebrews because their widows were being neglected in the daily distribution" (Acts of the Apostles 6:1).

The Apostles knew that they needed to change the situation. However, they also sensed that the time they would spend organizing and administrating these works of charity would take away from their true vocation of prayer and ministry of the Word. As a solution they delegated these works of charity to other faith-filled men.

© Bill Wittman/www.wpwittman.com

Most deacons are not full-time Church ministers. They earn their living by working in the world, just as most of the laity does. Are you familiar with any deacons who are serving in your parish?

So the Twelve called together the community of the disciples and said, "It is not right for us to neglect the word of God to serve at table. Brothers, select from among you seven reputable men, filled with the Spirit and wisdom, whom we shall appoint to this task, whereas we shall devote ourselves to prayer and to the ministry of the word." (Acts of the Apostles 6:2–4)

The Acts of the Apostles tells us that these seven men were chosen to oversee the sustenance of the community's poor, while the Apostles remained dedicated to prayer and to the ministry of the Word. These men were officially established in their new state and mission by prayer and the laying on of hands by the Apostles (see Acts of the Apostles 6:6). This was the beginning of the **diaconate** as we know it today.

Saint Stephen, the Church's first martyr, was one of the original seven deacons ordained by the twelve Apostles. Saint Lawrence (d. 258), another celebrated early deacon-martyr saint, is commemorated at Mass when "Eucharistic Prayer I" is prayed. Early bishops depended on their deacons for a number of functions, from the administration of the Church's temporal goods to assisting at Mass and other liturgies. In many ways the early deacons were their bishops' right hand men. The same is true today. Deacons are ordained to serve the bishops and priests in ministry to the People of God.

diaconate
The vocation and ministry of a deacon.

Saint Lawrence the Deacon

As a deacon in Rome in the third century, Saint Lawrence was responsible for maintaining the Church's material wealth and for managing that wealth wisely in order to help the poor in whatever way possible.

A tale says that prior to Saint Lawrence's martyrdom, the Roman emperor asked him to hand over the Church's riches to the Roman government authorities. Saint Lawrence replied that it would take some time for him to gather these riches all together. The emperor gave him time to do this.

After selling all the Church's gold and silver and using it for works of charity, he brought the poor, the sick, the widowed, and the orphaned together in one place to show the emperor. Expressing the Church's love for all her members, especially those in most need, Saint Lawrence told the emperor that *they* were the Church's most valuable treasures.

Transitional versus Permanent Deacons

In the early Church, the ministry of the deacon was considered a crucial vocation in and of itself. Many men gave their entire lives to God and the Church through their service in the diaconate. But by the sixth century in the Roman, or Latin, Church, the diaconate was largely known primarily as a stage of preparation on the way to ordination to the priesthood.

The Second Vatican Council affirmed the importance of the diaconate in preparation for the priesthood but sought to restore it to its rightful place as a true and full degree of Holy Orders. The council decreed that although candidates for priesthood would still be required to be ordained first as deacons, men called to be deacons but not priests could be ordained for permanent ministry as a deacon.

The aim of the bishops at the Second Vatican Council was to restore to the Church the role that the order of the diaconate once played. Because of this we now speak of two categories of deacons: transitional deacons and permanent deacons. Transitional deacons are men who are candidates for priesthood but are first ordained and serve as deacons for at least six months before being ordained as priests. Permanent deacons are men who are called to be deacons on a lifelong basis.

Permanent deacons may be either celibate or married. Celibate deacons must be at least twenty-five years old, unmarried, and willing to commit to remaining unmarried throughout their lives. If a man who is already married is called to the diaconate, he may also be ordained into the ministry with—among other requirements—the consent

Catholic Wisdom

Sacramental Grace in the Diaconate

In the following quotation from Pope Saint John Paul II, we witness a reference to the servant nature of the ministry of the deacons within the Church:

In the diaconate an effort is made to carry out what Jesus stated about his mission: "The Son of Man had not come to be served but to serve and to give his life in ransom for many" (Mk 10:45; Mt 20:28). ("Deacons Are Called to a Life of Holiness")

of his wife. A deacon cannot marry following ordination; therefore if a married permanent deacon is widowed, he may not remarry.

Serving as a Deacon

Most married permanent deacons exercise their ministry of service within the context of their local parish. In many cases a parish deacon may run one of the parish's charitable or educational programs, such as the Saint Vincent de Paul Society or a Bible study group. A deacon may also help with the administration or record keeping of the parish office.

In the Latin Church, unlike the Eastern Churches, deacons are ordinary ministers of the Sacrament of Baptism and are also empowered to witness marriages. Often deacons will not only baptize children and assist at and bless marriages but also assist in preparing people to receive these Sacraments. Because deacons are also ordinary ministers of Holy Communion, they often take part in the traditional ministry of bringing Communion to those who are sick and those who are homebound.

Deacons are also called to certain kinds of liturgical service. At Mass a deacon proclaims the Gospel and may also be given permission to preach the homily. During the Liturgy of the Eucharist, the deacon assists the main priest celebrant in many ways. Among other things the deacon is able to hold the chalice at the elevation.

Finally, although deacons cannot celebrate Mass, they are able to preside at funeral services outside of Mass. By comforting the grieving in this way, they answer their fundamental call to service and the works of mercy. ✝

Part Review

1. What is Apostolic Succession?

2. What do we mean when we say that a bishop is endowed with the fullness of the Sacrament of Holy Orders?

3. Explain the symbolism behind the ring a bishop wears.

4. Why are priests called the coworkers of the bishop?

5. What are some of the differences between a diocesan priest and a religious order priest?

6. Briefly describe the central elements of the vocation of a deacon.

7. Is the permanent diaconate a new development in the Church? Explain your response.

Part 3

The Sacrament of Holy Orders

No one can simply decide on his own to become a bishop, priest, or deacon—the call to ordained life is a special call from God, confirmed through the ministry of his Church.

When God calls a man to give his life in service through ordained life, God always grants the man the grace and courage necessary to say yes to this vocation. Those who are called must be open to this grace and to the vocation. Additionally, the Church helps men to accept the call to ordained life by providing them with a program of spiritual formation, which helps them to understand and accept the commitment God is calling them to make.

Through the celebration of the Sacrament of Holy Orders, men are empowered to celebrate the Sacraments. The Sacrament of Holy Orders confers upon the ordained an indelible spiritual character. This is a seal or character, permanently marking the souls of the ordained. By being configured to Christ though the grace of the Holy Spirit, the ordained are in turn able to bring God's grace to the faithful in real and tangible ways.

The articles in this part address the following topics:

Article 28 Who May Be Called?

What are the qualifications of, and who exactly might be called to, ordained life? No one can decide on his own if he is called to Holy Orders. The vocation to ordained life is always a personal call from God but must also be confirmed by the Church.

Baptized Men

Although both men and women followed Christ as his disciples when he walked the earth, Christ called only men to become his Apostles. Following the example of Jesus, the Church calls only baptized men to ordained life.

When Christ gave his Apostles authority to continue his mission and ministry, he gave them the power to act as

© Bill Wittman/www.wpwittman.com

The Church leader you are probably most familiar with is the priest (or priests) of your parish. A parish priest is often a "people person" who enjoys meeting with his parishioners, sharing their joys and sorrows.

he did. And so, because Christ never called a woman to serve him as an Apostle, the Apostles and all of their successors have the power to ordain only men to the priesthood, episcopate, or diaconate. Simply stated, the Church does not have the authority to ordain women because Christ never gave the Church the power to do so. This practice is not a question of women's ability to carry out the functions of the ministry; rather, it is a matter of what Christ has established and the sacramental reality of the priestly office.

The traditional practice and teachings of the Church support the precedent of an all-male priesthood set by Christ himself. A bishop or priest serves *in persona Christi,* meaning "in the person of Christ": head of his Body, and the Bridegroom of the Church. This is why, throughout a two-thousand-year history, there is no record of the Church's ever having validly ordained a woman. Although there are references to female deacons in some early Christian writings, there is also no historical evidence that these "deaconesses" were a part of the ordained diaconate as we understand it today.

To some it might seem unfair that only men are called to Holy Orders. However, it is important to remember that the ordained priesthood is an undeserved gift from God, to which nobody can claim a "right." It is also important to note that the Church greatly values the gifts and contributions of women and considers them as having their own unique mission and vocation as members of the Body of Christ:

> The Church desires that Christian women should become fully aware of the greatness of their mission: today their role is of capital importance both for the renewal and humanization of society and for the rediscovery by believers of the true face of the Church. (*Declaration on the Question of Admission of Women to the Ministerial Priesthood [Inter Insigniores]*, 6)

Celibacy

Bishops, priests, transitional deacons, and permanent deacons who are unmarried or who are widowed are called to commit to a life of celibacy. This is another key characteristic of those the Church considers for ordained life. Men who are seeking ordained life are required to give themselves fully to God for the sake of the Kingdom with their whole, undivided heart.

The Church never forces anyone to embrace a life of celibacy. It does recognize, however, that God calls some men to remain unmarried. In her wisdom the Church has discerned that this level of courageous, single-minded devotion to God, the Church, and the Kingdom of Heaven is a quality that should be manifested in those whom she calls to Holy Orders. The Church has the right and the responsibility to ordain only those men whom she discerns to be most suitable. Because of this, the Church has a right to ask that candidates for ordination be willing to give their lives in commitment to celibacy, imitating Jesus Christ in his own chosen way of life.

The only exception to this requirement of celibacy among Roman Catholic clergy is in the case of permanent deacons. Permanent deacons may be called from among either married or celibate men. However, if a married deacon were to become a widower, that deacon cannot remarry, and would need to commit to living a celibate lifestyle from that point on.

Married Priests?

Though the Church highly values the call to celibacy, there are a few cases in which married men can become priests. For instance, it is the custom of the Eastern Catholic Churches to permit married priests. However, while an already-married man can be ordained a priest in the Eastern Church, a man cannot marry or remarry after having received the Sacrament of Holy Orders. Additionally, married Eastern Church priests are not eligible to become bishops.

In the Latin Church, married men can at times be ordained priests in very exceptional circumstances. If a married man converts to Catholicism after years of having served in the clergy of certain other Churches or ecclesial communities, such as the Anglican Church or the Greek Orthodox Church, he may receive special permission to be ordained as a Catholic priest while remaining within his marriage and family life.

Necessary Personal Qualities

In addition to the requirements of being a baptized man committed to living a celibate life, some other qualities and characteristics are helpful for those who are considering a vocation to ordained life. If you were to look at the vocations Web sites for some dioceses from around the country, you would find some of these qualities listed. Although the lists are not exhaustive, they point to characteristics that are important for effective and holy ministry as an ordained man.

A candidate for ordained life should have an age-appropriate degree of personal maturity. It is important that the person can relate well with others and enjoys being around people. He should have healthy, balanced relationships with men and women of all ages. He must be able to set priorities and understand the consequences of various actions, and he must be able to take responsibility for his decisions and actions.

A candidate for ordination should have an awareness of God's presence, an active prayer life, and a desire to talk about faith. He should understand that personal sacrifice may be necessary to accept the call to the priesthood or diaconate, and he must be ready to put the needs of other people before his own at times. He should have a sincere concern for the spiritual good of others and a desire to serve others.

Some of the other qualities that can be helpful for those considering ordained life include demonstrating solid leadership and collaborative skills, a high degree of personal integrity, a respect for all people, and an ability to empathize. Obviously no one is perfect and has all the skills and characteristics needed for serving the Church in ordained ministry; however, a candidate for ordained life should have strengths in a number of the areas mentioned and should be willing to work at developing all the needed skills and characteristics. ☩

© Bill Wittman/www.wpwittman.com

Priests utilize a variety of gifts and skills in their ministry. You can contact your own diocesan vocation office to see what qualities they suggest are helpful for those considering the priesthood.

Article
29 Preparing for the Priesthood

The word *formation* is sometimes used to describe the process of coming to a richer, deeper understanding and living out of one's faith. It can be applied to anyone growing in faith within the Church. It is also used to describe the process of preparation that candidates for the priesthood undergo.

Although academic studies and practical training are part of the formation process for the priesthood, formation goes much deeper than mere training or studying. Where a training program focuses on learning how to do something and a curriculum of studies focuses on what the student is to know in an intellectual way, formation involves becoming a certain kind of person.

During his papacy, Saint John Paul II, in a document titled *I Will Give You Shepherds (Pastores Dabo Vobis)* named four pillars that are essential in priestly formation: human formation, spiritual formation, intellectual formation, and pastoral formation. Human formation focuses on strengthening the natural virtues. Spiritual formation focuses on one's interior prayer life. Intellectual formation enables one to comprehend and articulate the mysteries of the faith. Pastoral formation has the goal of showing a person how to

priestly lifestyle. These four pillars are part of the standard process of formation that prepares men for the priesthood.

The process of formation for bishops is not formalized. However, because bishops are chosen from among the ranks of long-serving, faithful priests, a new bishop will have already had many years of "formation." His own earlier preparation for the priesthood and his years of priestly prayer and service are what prepare him for his new responsibilities as bishop.

Parents are the first proclaimers of the faith to their children. They teach their children the virtues and set a good example by their own lifestyle.

© wavebreakmedia ltd/Shutterstock.com

Family Life: The First Formation

Long before any formal steps are taken toward preparation for Holy Orders, a future priest receives his earliest formation at home, from his family. Of course, God can call anyone whom he chooses to serve him as a priest, regardless of whether he had a happy family situation when he was growing up. Still, for many priests, the first formation they receive is the formation that comes from being a part of a loving, healthy, Catholic family.

Boys who witness their parents' self-sacrificial, committed, and faithful love for each other can observe firsthand the same kind of love that is needed to stay faithful to a priestly vocation. Young men who see their parents' devotion to their children gain an understanding of the type of care and concern a priest should have toward

Live It!

Everyday Discipleship

Through Baptism all Christians are called to be Jesus' disciples in whatever path their lives take. In whatever you do, whether it is a part-time job at a fast-food restaurant, your schoolwork, or your participation in school athletics, remember that attitude is everything. If you have a job, do you approach it half-heartedly, or are you enthusiastic, always giving your best effort? Do you see school as a necessary evil to get a high-paying job, or do you see it as a preparation for a career that will allow you to serve others and contribute to society? In the sports you participate in, are you in the game just for yourself, or do you always work for the good and success of the whole team? Jesus is calling you to be formed as his disciple wherever you are and in whatever you might be doing.

the people in his care. And in families where prayer is a daily practice, a future priest can gain the foundation of a solid spirituality that will last him for the rest of his life.

Families can also play an important role by supporting a young man as he prayerfully considers whether God might be calling him to be a priest. The encouragement of parents, siblings, and other relatives can help a young man to find the courage to respond to a priestly vocation.

seminary
A school established for the formation of future priests.

The Seminary

When a man senses with a reasonable degree of certainty that God is calling him to be a priest, he often seeks the counsel and guidance of a vocation director. A vocation director is someone who helps people to discern their vocation. At some point a vocation director might encourage a man discerning the vocation to ordained life to apply to enter a **seminary**, a special school established for the formation of priests (and sometimes for permanent deacons). Men studying at seminaries are called seminarians.

Depending on his educational background, a future priest may spend between six and eight years in the seminary. The first two to four years are called pretheology seminary, or sometimes college seminary for those men who are completing undergraduate degrees. In pretheology, seminarians study philosophy, primarily to foster a love for seeking the truth but also to gain the critical thinking skills necessary to understand the complicated teachings of our faith. They also study Latin, the official language of the Catholic Church, and Greek, the language in which the New Testament was originally written.

The final four years of priestly formation are spent in the major seminary. The studies in the major seminary focus on theology—dogmatic theology (the study of the objective truths and teachings of our faith), moral theology (the study of what is good versus what is sinful), spiritual theology (the study of prayer and spirituality), and Sacred Scripture. Theological study helps to enrich a seminarian's relationship with God by enabling him to love and contemplate the truths of the faith more deeply. It also enables the seminarian to be able to explain the beliefs and teachings of the Church once he becomes a priest.

Formation for Permanent Deacons

Like priests, permanent deacons also go through a program of preparation that includes human, intellectual, spiritual, and pastoral formation. For a young celibate candidate for the permanent diaconate, this formation may be quite similar to the usual programs of priestly formation, including time spent in residence at a seminary. Older or married diaconate candidates usually take an abbreviated series of theology courses, often with flexible or weekend class schedules. If an aspiring permanent deacon is married, often his wife will participate in a period of formation as well.

© Bill Wittman/www.wpwittman.com

In addition to different focuses of theology, men may study Canon Law and Church history. They may also study subjects designed to help their future priestly ministry in practical ways, such as psychology or public speaking. Seminarians are taught the proper way to administer the Sacraments though hands-on or *practicum* classes.

Spiritual formation nurtures a seminarian's most important priority: deepening his communion with Jesus Christ. There are many ways in which seminarians are encouraged and nurtured in their spiritual formation. One way is through a commitment to various forms of personal and communal prayer. Students and faculty participate in daily Mass together and celebrate the Liturgy of the Hours in common. Seminarians also meet regularly with a spiritual director—someone who is trained to help them to grow in prayer though one-on-one conversations—and participate in a yearly time of retreat.

Seminaries also have programs of pastoral formation. These often involve supervised service assignments in which the seminarians gain experience working with many different kinds of people. Seminarians do activities such as visiting nursing homes and hospitals, teaching children's religious education classes, or helping in shelters or soup kitchens. In many places seminarians spend their summers assisting in local parishes. The goal of pastoral formation is to help to create priests who are "true shepherds of souls after the model of our Lord Jesus Christ, teacher, priest, and shepherd" (*Decree on Priestly Training [Optatam Totius]*, 4). ✝

dalmatic
The liturgical vestment proper to a deacon. A dalmatic is shaped like a large, loose tunic with sleeves.

Article 30 The Celebration of the Sacrament of Holy Orders

An important milestone in the journey to priesthood is ordination to the transitional diaconate. Seminarians are required to become deacons before they become priests. This is because the call to the diaconate is a call to service, and all priests must have a commitment to service as the foundation of their priestly life, vocation, and ministry.

At the beginning of a diaconate ordination, the candidates are typically seated among the people within the main body of the church or cathedral. After the Scripture readings, the candidates are called forward by the bishop into the entrance of the sanctuary. This signifies that the soon-to-be deacons will no longer be considered laypeople; they are instead entering into the state of the clergy. From that point on, they are to be dedicated to God in a special way.

Ordination to the diaconate is the time when a transitional deacon (or an unmarried permanent deacon) makes his promise of lifelong celibacy. Transitional deacons also promise at their ordination to pray the Liturgy of the Hours every day for the rest of their lives.

After the laying on of hands and the prayer of consecration—the essential rite that actually confers the Sacrament of Holy Orders—new deacons are assisted in putting on a stole and **dalmatic**, the vestment deacons wear at Mass. They are then handed the *Book of the Gospels* and given the commission of preaching. The new deacons may then be invited to assist at the altar during the Liturgy of the Eucharist.

Ordination to the Priesthood

An ordination to the priesthood usually takes place in the cathedral of a diocese to underscore the fact that a priest is a coworker with the local bishop. At the beginning of priestly ordination, transitional deacons are seated within the sanctuary. The bishop calls them each by name, and the transitional deacons make a response indicating that they are ready to accept the call to priesthood. Then a priest responsible for formation testifies to the bishop that the candidates for priesthood have been found worthy to be ordained. The assembled People of God also make some expression of their confidence in the candidates' vocation.

The bishop next questions the transitional deacons on their resolve to dedicate their lives to priestly service. They kneel before the bishop, promising their loyalty and obedience to him and his successors. Then the bishop invites all the clergy and people assembled to pray for an outpouring of the Holy Spirit upon the candidates. While the Litany of the Saints is sung or chanted, the candidates for priesthood lay facedown on the floor in the sanctuary, in

Lectors and Acolytes

Sometime after becoming candidates, seminarians are instituted as lectors and acolytes. A lector is one who is commissioned to read Scripture, with the exception of the Gospel, at Mass. An acolyte is one who assists at the altar.

Any baptized Catholics who live in accord with the Church's teachings are able to take on these roles within the bounds of their parish community. Perhaps you have even served as a reader or altar server at your parish. However, when a man is formally instituted as a lector or acolyte, he is given permission to practice these ministries at liturgical celebrations in any church.

front of the altar. This dramatic gesture shows their total surrender to God, their humility before his awesome power and might, and their willingness to imitate Christ by "laying down their lives" (see John 15:13) for God's people.

© Alessandra Benedetti/Corbis

Following the Litany of the Saints, the bishop lays his hands on each of the candidates' heads in silence. Then the bishop prays a solemn prayer of consecration. From this point on, and through all eternity, these candidates are now priests of Jesus Christ. As a sign of this, the new priests are clothed with a priest's stole and chasuble, the garments that priests wear to celebrate Mass.

The new priests' hands are anointed with Sacred Chrism, as their hands are now able to make Christ present in the Eucharist. At the offertory of the ordination Mass, the bishop places the paten and chalice in each of the new priests' hands with a prayer that he may worthily celebrate the Mass. Finally, the bishop gives each of his new priests the sign of peace.

Pray It!

An Ordination Prayer

One of the most beautiful prayers in the Rite of Ordination for priests is the prayer of the bishop as he hands the chalice and paten to the newly ordained priest: "Receive the oblation of the holy people, to be offered to God. Understand what you do, imitate what you celebrate, and conform your life to the mystery of the Lord's cross" (Rite of Ordination, 135).

This prayer reminds the new priest that his whole life is now to be one of constant self-giving—in terms of both his own gift of self to God and his vocation to help the rest of the faithful offer their lives to God. It also reminds us that our own lives can be offered to God in the celebration of the Eucharist. The next time you receive Holy Communion, reflect on the phrase "conform your life to the mystery of the Lord's cross" and ask God to help you to live these words.

Episcopal Consecration

After years of faithful service, some priests may be called to the fullness of the Sacrament of Holy Orders through ordination as a bishop, which is also called episcopal consecration.

Only the Pope can decide to ordain a new bishop; therefore at the beginning of an episcopal ordination, the principal consecrating bishop ceremonially asks that the letter from the **Holy See**, which appointed the bishop-elect, is shown to all the people present.

After this, just as in priestly and diaconate ordinations, there is an examination of the bishop-elect's willingness to undertake faithfully the duties of his new calling, the praying of the Litany of the Saints, and a laying on of hands. There must be at least three bishops present in order to ordain a new bishop, and each of the three lays hands on the bishop-elect. Any other bishops in attendance do so as well.

During the prayer of episcopal consecration, the *Book of the Gospels* is held open over the head of the bishop-elect. Then the new bishop's head is anointed with Sacred Chrism, and the *Book of the Gospels* is handed to him. After this he is given the **insignia** of his office as bishop: the ring, the miter, and a crozier. ✝

Holy See
This term is a translation of the Latin *sancta sedes,* which literally means "holy seat." The word *see* refers to a diocese or seat of a bishop. The Holy See is the seat of the central administration of the whole Church, under the leadership of the Pope, the Bishop of Rome.

insignia
Signs and symbols of one's office, ministry, or vocation.

The essential elements of the Sacrament of Holy Orders are the laying on of hands and the speaking of the prayer of consecration.

© P Deliss/Corbis

Article 31   The Effects of the Sacrament

What happens to a man when he receives the Sacrament of Holy Orders? On the outside there may not be much observable difference. But when a man is ordained, his soul is forever changed. Ordination marks a man with a permanent seal or character.

What Is a Sacramental Character?

The Sacraments of Baptism, Confirmation, and Holy Orders all confer an indelible spiritual character. This means that they leave a permanent seal or an indelible mark on a person's soul, fundamentally changing the recipient's identity. Because such Sacraments create a dramatic spiritual change, a person can receive them only once in a lifetime.

Baptism and Confirmation are Sacraments of Christian Initiation and, therefore, confer the character of belonging to Christ in a special way. They mark us as people who are incorporated into Christ's Body, the Church, and who have been redeemed from our sins as the adopted sons and daughters of God. Because God creates every human being in his image and likeness, everyone—baptized or not—has innate dignity from the moment of conception. However, in Baptism, through the power of the Holy Spirit, we become part of God's family as his adopted children.

The Donatist Heresy

The Church was prompted to articulate clearly the teaching on the efficacy of the Sacraments in response to a movement in the early Church called Donatism, or the Donatist heresy.

The Donatist heresy found its roots in the historical circumstances of the Church in the early fourth century when the Roman persecution of Christians was particularly brutal. At the time many Christians chose to die as martyrs rather than deny their faith, reveal the names of other Christians to the Roman authorities, or turn over sacred objects (such as copies of Scripture or the vessels used at Mass). However, some other Christians, fearing torture or death, caved in to the pressure wielded by their persecutors. Once the persecutions subsided, many of the Christians—including some of the clergy—who had once denied their faith out of fear now wished to return to the Church.

The official position of the Church was that truly repentant sinners would be welcomed back and that the Sacraments administered by penitent clergy who had denied Christ would indeed be valid. In contrast the Donatists believed that the sin of denying Christ made a priest or bishop not only forever unworthy but also permanently unable to administer the Sacraments. Saint Augustine of Hippo helped put an end to this controversy in his writings wherein he expounds on the Church's teaching that the validity of the Sacraments depends on the holiness of God rather than on the personal holiness of the individual priest.

Each of the three degrees of Holy Orders also confers a character. Once a man is ordained, he is forever marked as one specially called and set apart for God's service. Through ordination a man is configured to Christ in a particular way and serves as Christ's instrument and representative for the Church.

The Grace of the Holy Spirit

The grace of the Sacrament of Holy Orders is union with Christ and being given a share in his mission as Priest, Teacher, and Pastor. The special grace of this Sacrament for the bishop is the grace of strength—strength to govern and guide; strength to love all, especially those in need; and strength to proclaim the Gospel to all. He is given strength to be a role model for his people, to walk the way of holiness ahead of them as a shepherd leads his flock, and to lead them to the life-giving Eucharist, in which he identifies with Christ. In this Sacrament he is given strength to give his life, day by day, for his sheep.

A prayer from the Byzantine liturgy expresses the grace of this Sacrament for priests. In this rite the bishop, while laying his hand on the priest, prays to the Father that the new priest may be filled with the Holy Spirit:

> That he may be worthy to stand without reproach before your altar,
>
> to proclaim the Gospel of your kingdom,
> to fulfill the ministry of your word of truth,
> to offer you spiritual gifts and sacrifices,
> to renew your people by the bath of rebirth.
> (*Catechism of the Catholic Church [CCC]*, 1587)

The prayer continues with the petition that the priest may, at the second coming of Christ, meet our Savior Jesus Christ and receive a just reward for "a faithful administration of his order"[4] (*CCC*, 1587).

The sacramental grace for deacons is a whole-hearted commitment to the People of God. In this commitment deacons cooperate with the bishop and priests, offer service in the liturgy, proclaim the Word of God, and reach out in works of love toward those who are in need.

The grace of ordination, as all graces, requires the cooperation and continual conversion of the one who receives it.

Grace is a gift. It is not a thing but a relationship. The closer the bishop, the priest, and the deacon come to God, the more faithfully they will live out their commitment to serve God's people. The ordained clergy are ordained not just as leaders, but as servant leaders, following in the footsteps of Christ. They are ordained to help the People of God to follow their own baptismal call—to follow Christ in the path of their own vocations. In this the ordained ministers can have no greater model of service than Jesus, the Good Shepherd, who gave up his life for his sheep.

A Permanent Change

Once a man becomes a priest, he is "a priest forever in the manner of Melchizedek" (Psalm 110:4). Because Holy Orders confers a special character, ordination is permanent. It is not possible to "un-ordain" anyone who has received Holy Orders. A deacon, priest, or bishop can never truly go back to being a layman.

It is true that in some very serious, rare, and unexpected difficult situations, a deacon, priest, or bishop can personally request a dispensation from the rights and obligations of his clerical state, or the Church may dismiss him from these rights and obligations after a canonical proceeding. This means that he will no longer be required or allowed to function as a priest. However, laicization—that is, leaving the life of ordained ministry, either by an ordained minister's own request (dispensation) or as a penalty imposed by the Church (dismissal)—does not mean his ordination is invalid.

Catholic Wisdom

A Change in Being

John Cardinal O'Connor, the late Archbishop of New York, describes the nature of the priesthood this way:

> A man is not merely invited to put on a set of vestments or authorized to serve in a particular capacity, with the new title of "Father." He *becomes* a priest. A [spiritual] change takes place in his very being, so that while he looks and walks and talks as before, now he *is* a priest. (In Fr. Benedict Groeschel, *A Priest Forever: The Life of Father Eugene Hamilton*, page 9)

He may be permitted or required to live as a layman, but his soul still bears the character of the priesthood, the indelible mark he received through the Sacrament of Holy Orders that no one can take away. Because of this, even a man who leaves the active priesthood can still grant absolution in the Sacrament of Penance and Reconciliation in an emergency situation in which there is danger of death. ♱

Part Review

1. How is formation for ordained life different from a program of study at an ordinary college or graduate school?

2. Briefly describe what is involved in the formation for the priesthood.

3. Why does the Church ordain only men?

4. Why is celibacy a requirement for priests?

5. Describe some of the main elements of the ritual for ordination to the diaconate, priesthood, and episcopate.

6. What does it mean to say that ordination is permanent?

Consecrated Life

Part 1

Understanding Consecrated Life

Consecrated life is a special vocation in the Church, one in which men and women freely offer their entire selves to Christ in response to a call from God through the Holy Spirit. A vocation to consecrated life is a commitment to seek to conform one's life to Christ more deeply and to give oneself totally to God. Men and women in consecrated life witness, in a unique way, to the coming of the Kingdom of Heaven.

The consecrated life is its own category within the Church and is not in itself part of the Church's hierarchical structure, although consecrated men in many religious orders are also ordained clergy. Though there are a variety of ways to live out the call to consecrated life, it is universally characterized by a permanent profession of the evangelical counsels of poverty, chastity, and obedience, in a stable form of life recognized by the Church.

There have been consecrated men and women since the very beginning of the Church. The consecrated life is an essential part of the Church's life and holiness.

The articles in this part address the following topics:

Article 32 Living the Evangelical Counsels

What is **consecrated life**, and what does it mean to be consecrated? The word *consecrated* means "set aside for a sacred purpose." In our lives as Catholics, we encounter many different examples of consecration.

consecrated life
A state of life recognized by the Church in which a person publicly professes vows of poverty, chastity, and obedience.

For instance, Church buildings are consecrated because they are to be used for divine worship. The chalice used during the Liturgy of the Eucharist is consecrated—it is never to be used as an ordinary cup but only for the offering of the Eucharist. Cemeteries are consecrated places, and visitors are expected to demonstrate appropriate respect for the faithful departed. And the central action of the Mass is called the consecration: at that moment, the Eucharistic gifts are no longer ordinary bread and wine but become the most sacred Body and Blood of Jesus Christ.

In Baptism we are consecrated as Christians—that is, our baptismal consecration sets us apart from the power of sin and darkness and calls us to rise above the empty values and false ideals that the world often sets before us. Our Baptism consecrates us in a real way because it gives us a new identity as adopted members of God's own family. We are made into "a chosen race, a royal priesthood, a holy nation, a people of his own" (1 Peter 2:9).

Through our Baptism, then, all of us are consecrated to Christ and called to our fundamental Christian vocation of perfect charity with God and one another. However, God also calls some men and women to be consecrated to him even more intimately. When we speak of consecrated life as a distinct vocation within the Church, we are referring to those members of the faithful who are called to have the Church set them apart for God above and beyond the call we all receive at Baptism. Consecrated people give their lives entirely to Christ in a way that is not possible or proper for the vast majority of the laity. Their intense focus on God leads them to give up a number of legitimate earthly goods so that they can be even more fully given over to the things of Heaven.

© Atlantide Phototravel/Corbis

Different Kinds of Commitments

The ideal of a life consecrated to God has remained constant throughout the Church's history, but the commitment to consecrated life has been expressed in slightly different ways at different times. The Church today names the evangelical counsels as poverty, chastity, and obedience, but this description of the obligations of consecrated life dates only to the Middle Ages.

All men and women in consecrated life are indeed called to live out the counsels of poverty, chastity, and obedience. But some religious orders live out the evangelical counsels while taking slightly different vows. For example, Benedictine nuns and monks—whose order was founded in the sixth century—vow to live lives of obedience, stability, and conversion of life. As you have read, the vow of obedience is one of the evangelical counsels. Saint Benedict also required the monks and nuns of his order to vow stability—that is, to remain in the same monastic community for the rest of one's life under ordinary circumstances, unless one is called to help to begin a new monastery. The vow of stability includes accepting the counsel of poverty in common life. The third Benedictine vow, conversion of life, is a promise that the monk or nun will always strive to fulfill the high calling of his or her monastic vocation, including the counsel of chastity. Thus, although two of the Benedictine vows are worded in a slightly different way, they still encompass the evangelical counsels of obedience, poverty, and chastity.

Similarly, Dominican friars and nuns vow only obedience. However, this one vow covers their entire way of life, including the counsels of poverty and chastity as described in the rules of their order.

Those who are consecrated, aided by the grace of God, also seek to imitate Christ's own way of life as closely as possible. By striving to take on Christ's single-minded devotion to the accomplishment of the Father's will, consecrated people strive to offer every single aspect of their lives to God as a pleasing sacrifice.

The general category of consecrated life includes religious sisters, religious brothers, and priests who are part of religious communities. You may know men and women in consecrated life from your parish or school. Consecrated life also encompasses the contemplative monks and nuns who live hidden lives dedicated entirely to prayer. Other, perhaps less familiar, forms of consecrated life include the eremitic life, consecrated virginity, and secular institutes, which will be explored shortly.

evangelical counsels

The call to go beyond the minimum rules of life required by God (such as the Ten Commandments and the precepts of the Church) and strive for spiritual perfection through a life marked by a commitment to chastity, poverty, and obedience.

The Vows of Consecrated Life

The Church teaches that the vocation of consecrated life requires a permanent commitment to live according to the vows of poverty, chastity, and obedience. These vows are also known as **evangelical counsels**. The evangelical counsels are evangelical because they come directly from the life and teaching of Jesus in the Gospels. They are called counsels because they represent advice or guidance from Christ that is proposed to all disciples; they are ways to perfect the Christian life by removing all that stands in the way of charity. Though everyone is called to Christian holiness and the perfection of charity, some are moved by the Holy Spirit in a special way to profess these vows and to practice the evangelical counsels within a permanent state of life.

The Meaning of the Three Evangelical Counsels

The evangelical counsel of poverty is a call to imitate the material poverty that Christ experienced while he walked the earth, as well as the poverty of spirit that he advocated in the Beatitudes (see Matthew 5:3). Thus, this evangelical counsel recommends that we detach ourselves from wealth and material goods. Instead, we are to cultivate physical and spiritual humility and recognize our dependence on God. In religious life, the counsel of poverty can mean renouncing personal ownership of property to embrace communal ownership and the sharing of resources. In this way, those who commit to a life of evangelical poverty demonstrate that their true treasure is in Heaven (see Matthew 6:20).

The evangelical counsel of obedience means that consecrated people promise to accept God's will in place of their own—it is a call to imitate Christ's own obedience to the Father. True obedience must never violate natural law or the promptings of a well-formed conscience. For a consecrated person, obedience also means obeying one's lawful superiors in religious life, as well as the teachings of the Magisterium. Obedience involves a deep trust in the goodness of God's plan. Through obedience men and women in consecrated life are able to "lay down their lives" for their brothers and sisters in Christ (see John 15:13) by giving the needs of the Church first priority.

The evangelical counsel of chastity obliges consecrated people to remain chaste and unmarried "for the sake of the kingdom of heaven" (Matthew 19:12). Although different forms of consecrated life observe the counsels of poverty and obedience in slightly different ways, all ways of living a consecrated life are built upon celibate chastity. Every Christian is called to live the virtue of chastity in a way that is appropriate to his or her state in life, but consecrated men and

Live It!

The Evangelical Counsels: Are They for Everybody?

Laypeople by definition are not called to make public vows to observe the evangelical counsels even though these counsels are relevant to the lives of all Christians in other ways and are part of our baptismal call to holiness.

For those who are called to married life, the evangelical counsel of chastity entails fidelity to one's spouse and openness to children, a gift from God. For those who are single, chastity means avoiding sexual activity outside of marriage. Laypeople are also called to live the evangelical counsel of poverty by generously sharing their gifts, avoiding the sin of greed, and refusing to make material things the center of their lives—instead cultivating the humility and poverty of spirit to which Christ calls us in the Beatitudes (see Matthew 5:3). And all Catholics are called to live the counsel of obedience by allowing themselves to be guided by the Pope, together with their bishops and priests.

Take some time to consider how you might be called to live the evangelical counsels in your own life right now.

women vow to remain unmarried and to abstain from sexual intimacy. In doing so they make a free choice to sacrifice the possibility of marriage and family life.

Why would God call anyone to give up something so good and valuable as a spouse and children and accept the call to celibacy? It is important to understand that celibacy is not a call to love *less*—it is a call to love *more*. The call to love God with an undivided heart overflows into a call to love everyone whom God loves. Men and women in consecrated life, therefore, do have a family to love: the entire Church.

Although those who commit to a life of celibacy are not immune to feelings of loneliness at times (in fact, people in all states of life can experience this feeling), they generally live happy and fulfilling lives. Sexual intimacy is not a necessary requirement for happiness. By entering into the commitment to celibacy for the sake of Christ and the Kingdom of God, one is given the grace to live that commitment. The result is often an experience of consolation that cannot fully be understood by those who have not lived this commitment. ☩

Article

33 Consecrated Life in the Church

The consecrated life is essentially a vocation to love: to love God unselfishly with one's whole heart and to let this love overflow into love of one's neighbor. This love is a source of inspiration for the whole Church, and it contributes to the Church's vitality and strength. The love represented by vocations to consecrated life helps to animate and encourage both the lay faithful and the Church's ordained ministers.

As a result, consecrated life provides one avenue for God to accomplish his will through the Church. Like Mary, whose "yes" opened the way for the Incarnation, men and women in consecrated life freely respond to God's grace in a way that allows him to bestow his gifts and blessings upon all his people.

This fresco of Saint Francis of Assisi by Giotto is titled "The Apparition at Arles." It is located in the Basilica of Saint Francis, in Assisi, Italy. What can you recall about the life of Saint Francis of Assisi?

© Elio Ciol/CORBIS

We can see this principle in action throughout the Church's history. In the third, fourth, and fifth centuries, the hidden penitential life of the desert hermits moved the Church toward a deeper appreciation of the importance of prayer and the interior life. The witness of religious founders like Saint Francis, Saint Clare, and Saint Dominic reminded the Church of the beauty of Christ's poor, chaste, and obedient way of life. And later religious communities dedicated to works of charity, such as the Society of Saint Vincent de Paul and the Daughters of Charity, have emphasized our Christian obligation to care for all of our brothers and sisters in need.

Examples of Faith

As the clergy are images of Christ, men and women in consecrated life are special signs of the mystery of redemption and encourage the larger Church by their example.

Consecrated men and women are called to be totally and absolutely given over to God in the same way the Church is given over to Christ, her bridegroom. Because of this, men and women in consecrated life can help us to better understand the nature of the Church. Consecrated men and women work for the benefit of the Church in a public way and are called to pray unceasingly on the Church's behalf. Through these gifts, consecrated people become examples of faith.

Consecrated Life and the Hierarchy

The hierarchy of the Church, like the Church in general, needs the gifts of love and witness found in consecrated life. In turn, the consecrated life also depends on those in the Church's hierarchy.

charism
A special gift or grace of the Holy Spirit given to an individual Christian or community, commonly for the benefit and building up of the entire Church.

Although all Christians are called to practice the evangelical counsels in ways appropriate to their vocation, it is only through the authority of the institutional Church that consecrated persons can be considered consecrated. Consecrated life is, by definition, a state in life that is established by the "competent authority of the Church" (*Code of Canon Law*, 573.2). For example, in religious orders and other communal forms of consecrated life, members vow or promise obedience to a particular way of life or set of constitutions. But a community's way of life must be approved by a representative of the Church's hierarchy before its members can officially call themselves consecrated persons. Additionally, in other forms of consecrated life, it is the local diocesan bishop himself who receives individuals into the consecrated state.

In short, it is only by the authority of the Church that baptized men and women can be formally set apart for God in the vocation of consecrated life. Because the clergy are ordained to stand in the place of Christ, the hierarchical Church acts on behalf of Christ by accepting the vows or other sacred bonds professed by consecrated persons.

The Church and the Discernment of Charisms

Consecrated life is a result of the direct workings of the Holy Spirit—that is, the Holy Spirit not only inspires men and

Catholic Wisdom

The Charity of God

The *Catechism of the Catholic Church* speaks of the value of religious life in all its forms:

> Religious life derives from the mystery of the Church. It is a gift she has received from her Lord, a gift she offers as a stable way of life to the faithful called by God to profess the counsels. . . . Religious life in its various forms is called to signify the very charity of God in the language of our time. (926)

women to follow Christ through the vocation of consecrated life, but also moves some to pursue their vocation focused on a particular **charism**. The charism given to a founder of a religious community is expressed and made evident through his or her particular spirituality and way of life. Those who join religious communities are called to live a life consecrated to God in the pattern set by a founder, according to the charism the founder received.

Because each founder receives a unique charism, every religious community has a specific mission within the Church. For example, the Institute of the Brothers of the Christian Schools, often simply referred to as the Christian Brothers, was founded by Saint John Baptist de La Salle for the purpose of educating the young. Blessed Teresa of Calcutta's religious community, the Missionaries of Charity, was founded for the purpose of offering loving service to the poorest of the poor.

A charism is a gift from God, so the Church's hierarchy cannot create a charism through human initiative. However, bishops are charged with discerning the validity of a charism. The Holy Spirit guides the Church to recognize God's workings, especially with regard to consecrated life. When the Holy See approves a new religious community— or even an entirely new form of consecrated life—it confirms that a particular inspiration within consecrated life is truly from the Holy Spirit. ✝

Article 34 A Sign of Heaven

Popular culture often portrays Heaven as something like an unending vacation with all the pleasures we enjoy on earth, and without the pain, struggle, or boredom of earthly life. More comical references to Heaven have Saint Peter standing at the "pearly gates," with the inhabitants of Heaven spending their days wearing white robes, sitting on clouds, and playing harps.

We know that Heaven is more profound than what is portrayed in the movies or on television. It is a place of perfect joy, because it is a place of union with God. The splendor of Heaven far surpasses the goodness of even the best and most beautiful things we experience in this life, placing

Heaven beyond our ability to understand. As Saint Paul reminds us in his First Epistle to the Corinthians, "What eye has not seen, and ear has not heard, / and what has not entered the human heart, / [is] what God has prepared for those who love him" (2:9).

However, the obscurity of heavenly realities can at times be a stumbling block to our growth in faith. We may have trouble seeing Heaven as relevant to our daily lives because it can seem so distant and hard to understand. And although we try to choose to do what is necessary to enter into Heaven one day, sometimes we can find it hard to long for Heaven in an intentional or focused way or to desire Heaven as we might desire a good thing in this life.

The difficulty of understanding Heaven helps us to appreciate a vital purpose of consecrated life in the Church. Consecrated men and women, through their unique commitment to Christ, can show us what Heaven is all about.

eschatological
Having to do with the last things: the Last Judgment, the particular judgment, the resurrection of the body, Heaven, Hell, and Purgatory.

An Eschatological Sign

The Church often speaks of the **eschatological** nature of consecrated life and calls men and women in consecrated life to be eschatological signs by conforming their whole lives to Christ and by focusing more exclusively on the things of Heaven. The word *eschatological* comes from the Greek word *eschaton*, meaning "last." It refers to final or ultimate things, in particular God's plan for the conclusion of time. Christ's second coming and the Last Judgment are both eschatological events. Our own personal eternal destinies, especially our call to live eternally in the presence of God, also have a strong, inherently eschatological dimension, because each of us will undergo a particular judgment at the moment of death.

The vocation of consecrated life is also predominantly eschatological. Consecrated life is fundamentally oriented toward ultimate things. It points toward realities that transcend our earthly experience. To help us to understand, we must remember Saint Paul's gentle admonition that "the world in its present form is passing away" (1 Corinthians 7:31). This reminder acknowledges the reality that our earthly life, as good as it might be, cannot last forever.

"Last Judgment," by Marcello Venusti. This painting is based on the fresco by Michelangelo that is on the wall behind the altar of the Sistine Chapel in the Vatican.

© Alinari Archives/CORBIS

Saint Paul also sought to reassure us that the temporary nature of our earthly life should not be a cause for sorrow but instead should inspire us with Christian hope. In our spiritual journey as Catholics, we can look forward to a time when our experience with the temporary goods of this life will give way to a fullness of life that will last forever—in other words, we will trade what is short term for what is lasting.

All Christians are called to live with this truth in mind, but men and women in consecrated life are called to root themselves in the eternal in a unique way. Consecrated men and women willingly forsake many of the wonderful things this world offers so that they are free to set their hearts on Heaven more easily and more intently.

Saint Thérèse of Lisieux

Thérèse of Lisieux, also known as the "Little Flower," was born in Alençon, France, in 1873. While still a young girl, Thérèse longed to enter the Carmelite convent in Lisieux. When she was fifteen, the bishop gave permission, and she joined two of her older sisters there. Her life of prayer and work in the convent was hidden to others, but she became known to the world through her autobiography *The Story of a Soul*, published in 1899. The book was translated into many languages and became widely popular.

In the book she describes her life as the "little way"—a simple life of spiritual childhood, characterized by acknowledging one's spiritual poverty, living with complete confidence in God's love, and dedicating one's days to the practice of love. Thérèse's little way to holiness emphasizes great love rather than great deeds and has appealed to countless people seeking to be holy in the midst of ordinary life.

A short time before her death, Thérèse remarked that she would spend her time in Heaven trying to do good on earth. She was canonized in 1925 and recognized for her life, which led others to pursue "everyday" holiness and pointed others toward the ultimate goal of Heaven.

Several of Jesus' parables can help us to understand this dimension of consecrated life. In Matthew 13:44, Jesus tells the story of a man who discovers a treasure hidden in a field and promptly sells everything he owns so he can buy the field. In Matthew 13:45–46, Jesus tells a similar story of a merchant who came across a pearl that was so perfect and valuable that the merchant was willing to sell everything he owned to buy it. He knew that, despite the great cost, it was still worth having.

Both the pearl of great price and the hidden treasure represent the eternal joys of Heaven. Tied to the vocation to consecrated life, we might say that consecrated people can be seen as those who sell everything they have (see Matthew 19:21), as Christ commanded. In their case *everything* means giving their whole selves and embracing chastity, poverty, and obedience in order to follow Christ more closely.

Every Christian will eventually be asked to "sell every-thing" at the moment of death. We will all need to let go of our earthly lives to enter into the life of Heaven. What

Pray It!

Death Is Not an End

Quite often on the night before a funeral, a rite called the Vigil for the Deceased is held to pray for the person who has died. The opening prayer of this rite is a wonderful prayer that acknowledges our pain in losing a loved one and also cel-ebrates the hope of eternal life:

Lord our God,
[Death reminds us of] our human condition
and the brevity of our lives on earth.
But for those who believe in your love
death is not the end,
nor does it destroy the bonds
that you forge in our lives.
We share the faith of your Son's disciples
and the hope of the children of God.
Bring the light of Christ's resurrection
to this time of testing and pain
as we pray for [the deceased] and for those who love him / her,
through Christ our Lord.
Amen.

(*Order of Christian Funerals*, 72)

makes a consecrated person an eschatological sign is the fact that she or he chooses to give up ordinary life and strives to center everything she or he does on Christ. In doing so, consecrated men and women become for the whole Church vivid reminders of our common destiny. ✝

Article 35 A Call to Joy and Holiness

A call to consecrated life is a bit like falling in love. Although consecrated people give up all romantic relationships, the comparison is apt when we consider what occurs within the hearts of those called to give everything to God.

Men and women who enter consecrated life are drawn to bind themselves to God and feel compelled to proclaim their love of him to the world. The vocation to consecrated life demands great sacrifices, but the love that consecrated people experience—both from God and for God—makes even difficult sacrifices not only bearable but often joyous.

Consecrated life is a vocation oriented toward the good of the entire Church. The Church truly needs men and women to say yes to God's call to embrace the evangelical counsels. Two special purposes of consecrated life are to promote the joy of those consecrated and to foster their continued growth in holiness.

A Call to Joy

A life of poverty, chastity, and obedience is not a vocation without challenges. But this vocation is made possible by the grace of God.

Men and women in consecrated life are fully human, and they experience the full range of human emotions, such as sadness, loneliness, and frustration, along the way. However, even when facing tremendous difficulties, those who generously respond to a vocation to consecrated life often continue to have a deep sense of peace. Because they have given their lives completely over to God, he becomes their permanent and abiding source of strength.

The choice to focus one's life on the Creator of all good things can manifest happiness and joy in a person. Consecrated men and women, because of their deep love for

Through their desire to more closely follow Christ, members of religious orders witness to the union of Christ with the Church.

© Bill Wittman/www.wpwittman.com

Christ, often experience joy in knowing that they belong to Christ in a unique way. A joy of consecrated life also arises from the delight of giving everything to Christ, who first gave himself totally to us in a supreme act of love.

A Call to Personal Holiness

Consecrated life is also a call to grow in personal holiness through a closer imitation of Jesus Christ whose very life was a revelation of the Kingdom of God. The evangelical counsels reflect Christ's own chosen way of life while he walked the earth. We know, for example, that Christ, like his Blessed Mother, remained celibate throughout his life. Jesus never married—his bride was the Church he founded (see Ephesians 5:23, Revelation 21:9). In the Gospel of Matthew, Christ also describes himself as poor: "Foxes have dens and birds of the sky have nests, but the Son of Man has nowhere to rest his head" (8:20). And the New Testament has countless references to Christ's perfect obedience of the Father's will. Saint Paul describes Christ as "becoming obedient to death, / even death on a cross" (Philippians 2:8), and in the Gospel of Matthew, Jesus demonstrates his obedience when he prays the night before his Passion and death: "My Father, if it is possible, let this cup pass from me; yet, not as I will, but as you will" (26:39).

Observing the evangelical counsels also helps men and women in consecrated life to resist the tendency toward sin that we all have due to our fallen human nature. The evangelical counsels aim to cut off sin at its root. A commitment to evangelical poverty, for example, helps one to overcome the inclination to greed and unhealthy attachment to mate-

Consecrated Life and the Paschal Mystery

In being called to a life of spiritual joy and growth in holiness, consecrated people are called to conform themselves in a special way to Christ's Passion, death, Resurrection, and Ascension. Through these events Christ won for us our eternal salvation and reconciled God and humanity, thereby paving the way for our own journey toward eternal life. The Paschal Mystery is a central mystery of our faith, and all Christians are called to echo it in their lives. For instance, in Baptism, we truly die to sin in order to gain new life as adopted children of God.

© Fred de Noyelle /Godong/Corbis

Men and women in consecrated life are called to conform themselves to the Paschal Mystery in a unique way. Consecrated persons seek to unite themselves to Christ's redemptive suffering through lives of penance and sacrifice. In this way they help to provide "what is lacking in the afflictions of Christ on behalf of his body, which is the church" (Colossians 1:24).

Consecrated men and women are also called to "die to the world" (see Colossians 2:20) through their conscious choice to renounce or detach themselves from many of the good things of this earth—not because they naturally dislike the world, but rather because this allows them to embrace a new and higher kind of life. Just as Christ died and was raised from the dead to live a new, resurrected life, consecrated people seek also to live a life fully informed by the Resurrection.

rial things. The counsel of obedience helps to counter pride and the inordinate desire for power. And celibacy calls one to live out the counsel of chastity in a way in which one's undivided heart is given to God. ✝

36 Dedicated to Service

How do you think our modern society would look without the contributions of consecrated persons throughout history? The fact is that our culture would be vastly different. As an example, let's take a look at our modern educational system and the ways in which consecrated religious contributed to its origins and structure.

After the fall of Rome in the fifth century AD, monks were largely responsible for preserving Western cultural heritage. Monastery schools were established to provide education for children of the nobility, filling the void created by the collapse of civil structures. In monasteries across Western Europe, especially in Ireland, monks toiled tirelessly to copy by hand manuscripts containing the writings of the Church Fathers and Sacred Scripture, as well as the works of Aristotle and other important classical thinkers, preserving them for the learning of future generations.

In the later Middle Ages, the university system developed in Europe under the direction of Dominican and Franciscan masters whose scholastic methods of learning and instruction attracted a growing number of followers. These gatherings of masters and students eventually developed into important universities, many of which remain to this day, and which provided the foundation of the modern university system.

In the modern era, many teaching orders, such as the Christian Brothers and the Ursuline Sisters, were

Do you know someone who is living the vocation of consecrated life? If so, take some time to ask them about their vocation and what it is like to live this state of life.

© Bill Wittman/www.wpwittman.com

corporal works of mercy

Charitable actions that respond to people's physical needs and show respect for human dignity. The traditional list of seven works includes feeding the hungry, giving drink to the thirsty, clothing the naked, sheltering the homeless, visiting the sick, visiting prisoners, and burying the dead.

spiritual works of mercy

Charitable actions that respond to people's spiritual needs and show respect for human dignity. The traditional list of seven works includes sharing knowledge, giving advice to those who need it, comforting those who suffer, being patient with others, forgiving those who hurt you, giving correction to those who need it, and praying for the living and the dead.

founded, many of them with a special mission to provide education to those who are poor. For centuries the only educational institutions in Europe were those established and run by those in religious life. Later, in the United States, men and women religious established schools in all parts of our nation, serving, among others, Native Americans and the children of immigrants. Such parochial schools continued to thrive in our country, and through much of the twentieth century, the vast majority were staffed entirely by religious sisters or brothers.

In addition to their contributions to education, men and women religious have contributed to our society and culture throughout history in other countless ways. We can feel their influence today in health care, care for the poor and oppressed, music and art, science and economics, and in many other areas. Take time to learn more about the many ways in which the work of religious sisters and brothers, nuns, priests, and monks influences our world today.

Being versus Doing

Because men and women in consecrated life continue to dedicate their lives to good works, many people mistakenly believe that a vocation to consecrated life is merely a call to join the Church's "workforce"—that is, they tend to equate the worth and purpose of consecrated life in the Church with the charitable work that consecrated people carry out, such as teaching in parish schools or providing assistance to those who are poor. Even though consecrated men and women have long been involved in important, much-needed, and often heroic works of charity, it is important to remember that the consecrated life is not primarily a vocation to do good deeds.

All Christians are called to engage in the **corporal works of mercy** and the **spiritual works of mercy**. Because of their special vocation, men and women in consecrated life have an even more pressing obligation to engage in the works of mercy. But it is also important to remember that the consecrated life is not so much a call to do good things as it is to become a certain kind of person—to wholly and completely give oneself over to God and his Church.

Certainly, men and women in consecrated life are also called to serve the Church in concrete ways. But their apos-

Blessed Mother Teresa

Blessed Mother Teresa was a woman of great faith. She was born Gonxha Agnes Bojaxhiu in 1910 in Skopje, Macedonia. At age eighteen, she joined the Sisters of Loreto and took the name Teresa after Saint Thérèse of Lisieux. After some time in Ireland to learn English, she moved to India where she was a schoolteacher and then a principal. After serving there for almost twenty years, Teresa experienced a call from God that led her to the service of those who suffered from the most extreme poverty.

© Reuters/Corbis

In 1948, through prayer and persistence, Mother Teresa received permission to leave her convent to work with the poorest of the poor in the streets of Calcutta. She was joined by former students and sought to found the Missionaries of Charity as an order dedicated to helping the poor. In 1950 the Church first recognized the Missionaries of Charity as an approved religious institute in Calcutta, and the sisters began to establish hospitals and homes for the dying in India. In 1979, after years of dedication to her mission, this "saint of the gutters" was awarded the Nobel Peace Prize for her work. By the 1990s the Missionaries of Charity could be found all over the world, helping homeless people, abused women, and orphans, as well as those suffering from AIDS, drug addiction, and other illnesses.

Mother Teresa died in 1997 and was beatified by Pope Saint John Paul II in 2002. She left behind a thriving religious order dedicated to prayer and devoted to the service of the neediest people in all parts of our world.

tolates, prayers, and active works of charity flow out of their identity as consecrated people. The good that they do is a direct result of who they are.

Prayer and Witness

Any consecrated person's most important work begins with prayer and witness to Christ in the world—that is, praying for the People of God and bearing witness to the primacy of Christ and the coming of the Kingdom of Heaven.

Of course, all Christians are called to prayer and witness in a way appropriate to their state in life. But consecrated men and women are given this obligation to a greater degree by virtue of their vocation. The degree of prayer and witness that can be achieved in a life consecrated totally to God is the specific contribution that consecrated men and women make to the life of the Church. So although laypeople can and do serve successfully in many of the ministries once held exclusively by religious, the consecrated life, with its ministry of prayer and witness, will always be a valuable and much-needed vocation within the Church. ✝

Part Review

1. Write a brief definition of the term *consecrated life*.

2. What are the evangelical counsels, and how are they a significant aspect of consecrated life?

3. Describe the role of consecrated life within the Church.

4. In what ways are the vocations of Holy Orders and consecrated life related?

5. What do we mean when we say that men and women in consecrated life are called to be eschatological signs?

6. Is consecrated life primarily a call to personal holiness or a call to the service of the Church? Explain your response.

Part 2

Different Forms of Consecrated Life

Each human being that God creates is unique. Although we all are called to live out our lives in response to God's love, no two people are called to do so in exactly the same way. God delights in giving his children a wide variety of gifts. As a result, even within the vocation of consecrated life, we find a number of different but equally valid paths.

The Church recognizes various forms of consecrated life today: consecrated virginity, the life of a hermit, religious life, societies of apostolic life, and secular institutes. The Church also remains open to new forms of consecrated life that might develop under the inspiration of the Holy Spirit.

The articles in this part address the following topics:

- Article 37: Consecrated Virgins (page 166)

- Article 38: Hermits (page 170)

- Article 39: Religious Life (page 173)

- Article 40: Societies of Apostolic Life (page 178)

- Article 41: Secular Institutes (page 181)

Article
37 Consecrated Virgins

During the Liturgy of the Eucharist, we sometimes hear the priest request the intercession of Saints Felicity, Perpetua, Agatha, Lucy, Agnes, Cecilia, and Anastasia. These female saints were martyrs who helped to build up the Church through the testimony of their lives and deaths.

Of these female martyrs, Saints Agatha, Lucy, Agnes, and Cecilia were also consecrated virgins—women called to renounce an earthly marriage in order to devote themselves more wholeheartedly to God through a spousal relationship with Christ. Today God continues to call women to follow the example of these four early virgin-martyr saints in the vocation of consecrated virginity.

© The Crosiers/Gene Plaisted, OSC

Saint Agnes lived in Rome, Italy, from c. 291–c. 304. This stained-glass window is in Saint Mary's Basilica in Phoenix, Arizona.

History of Consecrated Virginity

Consecrated virginity is the oldest form of consecrated life in the Church. The earliest mention of consecrated virgins as forming a distinct group within the Church can be found in Saint Ignatius of Antioch's Letter to the Smyrnaeans, written around the year AD 110.

In the First Letter to the Corinthians, Saint Paul writes that "an unmarried woman or a virgin is anxious about the things of the Lord, so that she may be holy in both body and spirit. A married woman, on the other hand, is anxious about the things of the world" (7:34). From the earliest days of the Church, some Christian women were willing to forgo marriage to instead dedicate themselves more wholly to Christ.

In the fourth century, Church Fathers such as Saint Ambrose, Saint Augustine, and Saint Jerome wrote extensive treatises on the vocation of consecrated virginity. Saint Ambrose gives us the first description of a liturgical ritual for the consecration of virgins when he recalls, in his work *De Virginibus* ("On Virgins"), his own sister's consecration. Our earliest surviving texts of the actual *Rite of Consecration to a Life of Virginity* are found in manuscripts from the sixth and seventh centuries.

The consecrated virgins of the first several centuries of the Church's history were neither contemplative nuns nor the active religious sisters more familiar to us today. Early consecrated virgins could not join religious communities because religious life as we know it did not develop until the mid-500s. Instead consecrated virgins lived "in the world," outside of monasteries.

Once the first religious orders in monasteries and convents were established, women religious would receive virginal consecration when they professed their final vows, or sometimes several years after. Eventually the practice of consecrating women religious living outside of monasteries fell into disuse, although several monastic traditions preserved the *Rite of Consecration to a Life of Virginity* itself for posterity.

In the twentieth century, the Second Vatican Council (1962–1965) sought to foster a renewal of the Church's ancient liturgical heritage. As part of this renewal, the vocation of consecrated virginity lived outside of a religious community was restored to the life of the contemporary Church.

The *Rite of Consecration to a Life of Virginity*

Today the *Rite of Consecration to a Life of Virginity* is the foundation of a vocation to consecrated virginity. A consecrated virgin is by definition a woman who has received the *Rite of Consecration*. (Women religious whose orders continue to use the *Rite of Consecration*, such as the Carthusian and some Benedictine orders, are consecrated virgins in addition to being nuns.) To validly receive the *Rite of*

Catholic Wisdom

Pope Benedict XVI Speaks to Consecrated Virgins

In 2008 consecrated virgins from around the world gathered together in Rome for an international pilgrimage. At a special audience with Pope Benedict XVI, the Holy Father addressed these words to those assembled:

> Take care always to radiate the dignity of being a bride of Christ, expressing the newness of Christian existence and the serene expectation of future life. . . . Be witnesses of attentive and lively expectation, of joy and of the peace that characterizes those who abandon themselves to God's love.

Consecration, a candidate must be a chaste Catholic woman who has never been married. Only a bishop can celebrate the *Rite of Consecration*.

Unlike those in religious life, consecrated virgins outside of religious orders do not follow the charism of any particular founder. Yet the *Rite of Consecration* itself contains a spirituality of its own, centered on a call to live as a bride of Christ. In renouncing marriage for the sake of the Kingdom of Heaven, a consecrated virgin offers Christ all the love she might otherwise have given to a husband and children. By entering into a spousal relationship with Christ, a consecrated virgin becomes a reflection of the Church herself.

The *Rite of Consecration to a Life of Virginity* always takes place during a Mass with many of the faithful in attendance. During the Liturgy of the Word, readings from the Old and New Testaments that highlight the spousal relationship between God and Israel and Christ and the Church are shared. After the Gospel the candidate is called into the sanctuary, often carrying a lit candle as a reminder of the wise virgins from the Parable of the Ten Virgins (see Matthew 25:1–13).

The celebrating bishop then preaches a homily reminding the assembly of the importance of the virtue of virginity in the life of the Church. Following prayers for an outpouring of grace in the Litany of the Saints, the candidate for consecration publicly renews her resolution to persevere in a life of virginity and service, which the bishop formally accepts in the name of the Church.

The most solemn part of the litany is the prayer of consecration, which the bishop recites over the candidate. After this the newly consecrated virgin is given a veil and a ring to symbolize her vocation as a bride of Christ.

Dedicated to the Local Church

Consecrated virgins are consecrated by the authority of the diocesan bishop, and they live out their vocation directly under his guidance. Because of this they have a unique and special bond with the local Church. Under normal circumstances the *Rite of Consecration* encourages diocesan bishops to celebrate the rite in the cathedral, and consecrated virgins often take part in the good works carried out by their diocese.

Consecrated virgins are called to live out a vocation to spiritual motherhood through prayer and apostolic work. During the *Rite of Consecration*, a consecrated virgin is presented with a **breviary** and is commissioned to pray for the needs of the world. Consecrated virgins pray the Liturgy of the Hours, maintain a faithful private prayer life, and receive the Sacraments regularly.

The *Rite of Consecration to a Life of Virginity* states that consecrated virgins "are to spend their time in works of

breviary
A prayer book that contains the prayers for the Liturgy of the Hours.

Dedicated Widowhood

Like consecrated virginity, the tradition of dedicated widowhood goes back to the earliest days of the Church. The New Testament frequently mentions widows as a distinct group within the Church. For example, Saint Paul sets out some guidelines for the conduct of widows in his First Letter to Timothy (see 5:3–16).

Because in the time of the early Church, widows were frequently not able to care for themselves, the newly established Christian communities attended to their practical needs (see Acts of the Apostles 6:1). As the "altars" on which the gifts of the faithful were offered to God in this work of charity, these widows were expected to live chaste, prayerful, and modest lives. In later centuries the Church Fathers would describe pious widows who chose to live semimonastic lives, dedicating themselves in a special way to prayer and penance.

Today men and women who have lost a spouse experience a deepening of their relationship with Christ as a result of their prayerful response to the solitude and suffering that comes from being widowed. Often these widows and widowers feel a call to dedicate the rest of their lives to Christ exclusively in a way that would preclude remarriage. They may then use the freedom inherent in their new state of life to allow themselves to spend more time in prayer and in service to the Church and the wider community.

penance and of mercy, in apostolic activity, and in prayer, according to their state in life and spiritual gifts" (2). Although they are called to dedicate themselves wholly to the service of the local Church, consecrated virgins are not automatically called to any particular apostolate; rather, a consecrated virgin engages in ongoing discernment with her bishop to identify how she can best use her gifts and talents to meet the needs of her diocese. ✝

Article 38 Hermits

© vitor costa/Shutterstock.com

The hermit tradition began around AD 250 with men who lived in the Egyptian desert. Though the hermit is alone, his or her prayer life is universal: he or she prays for the good of the whole world.

Hermits are baptized men and women who live alone in prayerful silence and solitude so that they can focus constantly on God, with as few distractions as possible. Contrary to common belief, hermits do not withdraw from human contact because they do not enjoy life and other people; rather, they choose to embrace a life of full-time, solitary prayer because they love God even more than all the good things of this world. In their total dedication to prayer, hermits witness to the world that Christ is everything to them. They are a sign—even if a hidden one—to the whole Church of the central importance of prayer and contemplation.

The Origins of the Eremitic Life

The vocation to eremitic life as a form of consecrated life emerged just as the early Roman persecutions of the Church were abating. Although the threat of persecution certainly endangered the early Church, this threat did have the positive effect of promoting fervor in the Christian community. Once the persecutions ceased, however, lukewarm spirituality started to become a more pressing pastoral issue within the early Church.

This shift was one factor in the emergence of the **eremitic** life. Some of the earliest hermits sought to live in isolation out of concern that they would waver in their commitment to Christ if they continued living among Christians who were less devout. As a solution they began to dwell in the desert or at the fringes of a city, seeking to maintain their fervor for Christ through an **ascetic** life of prayer and penance.

Additionally, once Christianity became legal in the Roman Empire, the chance of dying as a martyr also became far less likely. Thus especially devout Christians who continued to feel called to sacrifice their lives out of love for Christ chose what came to be called a white martyrdom—that is, they created a way of life in which they could "die to the world" and live for Christ alone.

eremitic
Relating to the life of a hermit, characterized by self-denial and solitude.

ascetic
Pertaining to spiritual discipline in which a person leads a strict life of simplicity and self-denial.

Hermit Saints

Saint Paul the Hermit (c. 230–342)
Saint Paul the Hermit fled into the desert at age fifteen, initially to escape persecution. He persevered in a life of prayer and penance until he died at the age of 112. Saint Paul is considered the earliest of the Church's hermit saints.

Saint Anthony of Egypt (c. 251–356)
Called the father of monks, Saint Anthony was the inspiration for numerous other hermits. We know a great deal about his life from a biography written by Saint Athanasius around AD 360.

Saint John Cassian (c. 360–435)
Saint John Cassian lived as a hermit for many years before being ordained a priest. He left us an extensive body of writing that we call his *Conferences*, which contains advice and guidance on the eremitic life. Many hermits and contemplative nuns and monks still find Saint John Cassian's writings relevant to their lives today.

The Early Hermits' Way of Life

lectio divina

A Latin term meaning "divine reading." *Lectio divina* is a form of meditative prayer focused on a Scripture passage. It involves repetitive readings and periods of reflection and can serve as either private or communal prayer.

Biographies of some of the early hermits, such as the biography of Saint Anthony of Egypt, can still be read today. There were also hermits who left spiritual writings on the proper way to live and pray within the vocation to eremitical life. As a result we know much about how the early hermits lived their consecrated lives, and we can trace the ways in which their spirituality has contributed to the life of the universal Church through the ages.

The early hermits lived a strict life of prayer, penance, and work. Their prayer, which was the main focus of their lives, took various forms. Many hermits memorized and recited the Psalms, for example, while those who could read often reflected deeply on Sacred Scripture in an early form of prayer we know today as **lectio divina**. To sanctify their time, hermits prayed at many different times throughout the day and often rose in the middle of the night to sing God's praises.

A hermit's life of penance was intended to make this life of prayer more fruitful. Often a hermit's penance involved physical austerity, such as sleeping on a hard bed or on the ground, fasting, staying awake in prayer for long hours at night, or wearing meager or uncomfortable clothing. However, the most important penance was found in the interior effort needed to stand fast against temptations to sin, which were abundant even in the solitude of the desert.

Live It!

Silence and Solitude

When you have to write a paper or study for a test, do you find that you need to turn off your music and the television and maybe even put a do-not-disturb sign on your door? Or when you want to pray, do you find it helpful to go someplace quiet, where you can be alone and avoid interruptions or distractions? If so, you have had a slight glimpse into what it means to have an eremitic vocation. Although relatively few Catholics are called to live the life of a hermit, it is good for all Christians to imitate the hermits once in a while by setting aside time to listen to God by praying in silence and solitude. Make some time today to be quiet with God. You might also consider taking an entire day or weekend to go on retreat, to experience what it is like to give God your undivided attention for a substantial period of time.

Through penance, hermits sought to love God to a greater degree by lessening their excessive attachment to anything other than God. Hermits aimed to free themselves from a too ardent desire for bodily comfort, for praise and esteem in the eyes of others, and for material riches. Most especially, hermits strove to free themselves from attachment to desires that led to sin.

cenobitic
Monastic life lived in community rather than in solitude.

Hermits Today

As formal religious orders developed starting in the sixth century, the eremitic life was gradually absorbed into **cenobitic**, or communal, monastic life. Rather than heading into the wilderness on their own, men and women who felt called to give themselves to God through a life of solitude gradually began to join religious orders that emphasized solitude as a characteristic of their communal life. Yet the spiritual roots planted by the early hermits continued to flourish. Many later religious orders, such as the Carmelites and the Carthusians, named the primitive eremitic life as their foundation and inspiration.

After Vatican Council II, the Church once more sought to recognize the vocation to eremitic life in its original form, apart from a religious community. When the *Code of Canon Law* was revised in 1983, it officially recognized the eremitic life of both men and women as a state of consecrated life.

Today modern hermits live under the direction of their local diocesan bishop. They usually make public vows of poverty, chastity, and obedience, which their bishop receives in the name of the Church. Hermits today also write their own "Rule of Life," a document that describes the concrete ways in which they intend to live out their vocation to solitary prayer. To support themselves hermits work at occupations that can be done from within their hermitage, such as skilled craftwork, icon painting, vestment sewing, or even web design. To discern a vocation to eremitic life, an aspiring hermit usually lives according to his or her proposed Rule of Life for several years before professing vows. †

Article 39 Religious Life

religious communities
A group of men or women religious who are joined by a common charism.

Religious life is probably the form of consecrated life most familiar to Catholics today. We often encounter men and women religious in schools and parishes, and many well-loved saints were members of **religious communities**.

Religious life has been part of the Church for nearly fifteen hundred years. Over the course of history, different religious communities have been founded in response to the Holy Spirit's promptings and the needs of the Church. Consequently, religious life takes on a wide variety of forms—from cloistered contemplative communities to active missionary communities.

History of Religious Life

The spiritual wisdom of Saint Benedict continues to lead more than twenty thousand monastic men and women. This stained-glass window is in St. Joseph Catholic Church in Springfield, Missouri.

© The Crosiers/Gene Plaisted, OSC

The earliest precursors to religious life were groups of consecrated virgins or hermits who lived together for mutual spiritual support in the Church's first few centuries. Christian monasticism is traditionally thought to have begun with Saint Anthony of Egypt (251–356), who led a life of prayer, meditation, and penance as a hermit in a desert cave in Egypt. Other hermits began to seek him out and took up their own lives of solitary prayer and penitence nearby. Over time the deserts of Egypt and Asia Minor began to see many such groups of monks following a spiritual leader. It was Saint Pachomius, a contemporary of Saint Anthony, who recognized that this movement needed some sort of order. Pachomius began to organize the first monasteries in 320. In the walled communities he organized, a group of men and women would live communally and follow a common rule that stressed prayer, celibacy, poverty, and obedience to a superior.

Religious life as we know it today began with the *Rule* of Saint Benedict, written around AD 529. Saint Benedict was originally a hermit living a solitary life dedicated to God. However, he soon attracted a number of followers and realized that for many a life of prayer and penance could be more fruitfully lived out in a supportive community. Influenced by the rule of life that

Saint Augustine had written in 400, Saint Benedict wrote his
Rule to guide his followers toward a communal way of life
that balances prayer and work. He founded several men's
communities based on the principles described in his *Rule*,
and his twin sister, Saint Scholastica, founded similar communities for women. For the next several centuries, religious
communities remained monastic in nature, meaning that
they were permanent, self-contained communities dedicated
primarily to contemplative prayer and liturgy.

mendicant
From a Latin root
mendicare, meaning
"to beg." Members
of mendicant orders
rely on charity for their
support.

In the later medieval period, the Holy Spirit led the
vocation of religious life in a new direction by inspiring the
mendicant orders. The mendicant orders, which include the
Franciscans and Dominicans, focused not only on prayer
and liturgy but also on apostolic activity. Mendicant friars
had a community life that retained many monastic elements,

Third Orders, Oblates, and Associate Members

Some baptized Catholics feel drawn to embrace the spirituality of a particular religious order or community but are called to remain in their lay state
rather than enter religious life. These men and women have the option to join
a Third Order or to become an oblate or an associate member of a religious
community. Members of Third Orders, oblates, and associate members can
be either married or single.

A Third Order is an organization for married or single laypeople who feel
called to share in the spirituality of one of the Church's religious orders. For
example, there are Third Order Carmelites, Franciscans, and Dominicans.
Third Order members usually meet regularly for fellowship and mutual support, commit to daily prayer practices that reflect the spirituality of their
orders, and receive spiritual advice from the priests and religious of the
order to which they are attached.

An oblate is a man or woman who feels called to a connection with a
particular contemplative monastery. Oblates typically commit to observing
the rule of the monastery to the greatest extent possible in accord with
their state in life and to receiving spiritual support and guidance from the
monastery.

An associate member of a religious community, like an oblate or a Third
Order member, feels called to integrate the spirituality and mission of a
particular religious community into his or her lay lifestyle. Associate members often join the religious community for prayer and celebration on special
occasions, and they volunteer their time to support the community's apostolate and service projects.

Counter-Reformation

A movement of internal reform within the Church during the later sixteenth and early seventeenth centuries that came about as a response to the Protestant Reformation.

but they also left their houses regularly to preach, teach, and engage in works of charity. Women in mendicant orders, such as the Franciscan Poor Clare nuns, continued to live enclosed monastic lives. However, their life of intercessory prayer also took on a new apostolic focus, as the nuns were specifically called to further the evangelical efforts of their brother friars though the support of their prayers and sacrifices.

During the Protestant Reformation in the sixteenth century and the subsequent **Counter-Reformation**, the Church's newly emerging spiritual and pastoral needs led to the founding of several new religious orders. It was at this time that Saint Ignatius of Loyola gathered the first members of the Society of Jesus, also known as the Jesuits, to combat distortion of Catholic doctrine through better education. Many early Jesuits were also active in foreign missionary work, bringing the Gospel for the first time to places in North America and East Asia.

In the seventeenth and eighteenth centuries, many congregations of "active" religious came into being. These noncloistered, nonmonastic communities combined a life of prayer with wholehearted dedication to charitable works. Today the religious communities that most people are familiar with and may recognize for their presence in parishes and schools are made up of men and women religious who belong to active communities.

Formation for Religious Life

After a period of careful, prayerful discernment, a man or woman aspiring to religious life will begin the process required to enter a religious community. Although not every religious community follows the same entrance process, many communities invite a candidate to enter a community as a postulant. The word *postulant* comes from the Latin word *postulare*, meaning "to ask." Postulants are asking their religious community to invite them to full membership at the same time that they are asking God if religious life is his will for them. During this time the postulants live with the community to discern whether God is truly calling them to religious life. Depending on the individual community, postulancy can last from a few months to one or two years.

If both the community and the postulant discern that the postulant continues to show strong signs of a religious vocation, the postulant is received into the community as a novice and enters a time of further formation that is called the novitiate. In some communities this is the point when the person aspiring to religious life receives a religious habit and sometimes also a new name. The focus of the novitiate is growth in prayer, study, continued discernment, deepening knowledge of the community's charism, and spiritual preparation for the profession of vows. The novitiate can last one or two years, with at least one full year devoted entirely to prayer and spiritual formation.

After completing the novitiate, the novice may ask to profess temporary vows. Men and women religious at this stage gradually take on more responsibilities within the community and may also continue academic or professional studies. Male religious who are called to the priesthood often attend seminary classes during their years of temporary profession. According to the laws of the Church, those in religious life must spend at least three years in temporary vows. In some communities temporary profession can last up to nine years.

Pray It!

Vow Formulas

Every order or congregation has its own vow formula, or prayer used in the act of professing religious vows.

Here is a portion of the vow formula that Saint Francis de Sales wrote for the nuns of the Order of the Visitation, a community he cofounded with Saint Jane of Chantal:

> O my God! To Thee I make the Vows of living in perpetual chastity, poverty, and obedience, according to the Rule of St. Augustine and the Constitutions of St. Francis of Sales, for the Congregation of our Lady of the Visitation: for the observance of which, I offer and consecrate to Thy divine Majesty, to the sacred Virgin Mary, Thy Mother our Lady, and to this Congregation, my person and my life.

Although we are not all called to profess religious vows, our Baptism calls each of us to live a life offered to God. If you had to write out a formula or prayer expressing your commitment to Christ, what words would you choose?

After the time allotted for temporary profession, these men and women religious may make final or perpetual vows. These bind them to their communities for life. Although final profession concludes the time of initial formation, men and women religious continually seek to grow and to be more deeply formed in their faith. ✞

Article 40 Societies of Apostolic Life

In 1633 Saint Vincent de Paul ran into a problem. Seeing the needs of the poor all around him, he felt it was God's will for him to establish a women's religious community dedicated to active works of charity. However, at the time the Church required that all women religious observe strict monastic enclosure.

It looked like a no-win situation. If the Daughters of Charity, the women's order Saint Vincent de Paul had founded with Saint Louise de Marillac, were going to serve the poor, then its members could not be cloistered and thus could not become women religious. Yet if the Daughters of Charity were to be established as a religious order, the laws of the Church would not allow them to do the very work for which they had been founded.

Saint Vincent de Paul's solution was to found the Daughters of Charity as a society of apostolic life, rather than a community of professed religious life. Instead of professing the lifelong vows of cloistered nuns, the Daughters of Charity would make temporary vows, to be renewed each year. This allowed them to lead a dedicated life, in a form recognized and approved by the Church, without being bound to observe the same restrictions as the cloistered nuns of their time.

Even though the Church no longer requires all women religious to be cloistered, to this day the Daughters of Charity continue their traditional practice of professing annual vows, and they are still classified as a society of apostolic life.

This painting of the Daughters of Charity distributing food to the poor, by Francois Bonvin, is from 1851. It is currently located in the Musee des Beaux-Arts in Niort, France.

What Is a Society of Apostolic Life?

A society of apostolic life is a form of consecrated life in which members unite around a common apostolic purpose, live in community, and observe the evangelical counsels but do not profess the vows common to religious life. However, members of societies of apostolic life make other kinds of commitments, such as promises, oaths, annual (temporary) vows, or some other **sacred bond**.

sacred bond
A binding commitment within the Church—especially to a particular state in life—that is recognized by Canon Law. Religious vows are considered sacred bonds, but a sacred bond does not necessarily need to be a religious vow. Other sacred bonds could include promises or oaths.

Societies of apostolic life are similar to apostolic religious life, and many were founded for the same reasons as some active religious communities. But because societies of apostolic life are distinct from institutes of religious life according to Canon Law, societies of apostolic life have more flexibility in structuring themselves.

For instance, all men and women religious are required to observe the evangelical counsel of poverty by renouncing their ability to own personal property. If a man or woman religious owns or gains any material good, it belongs legally to his or her community and not to the individual. In contrast, although members of societies of apostolic life are expected to live a simple lifestyle as a witness to the Gospel, in some cases they can own and manage their own property and goods.

Sometimes the type of commitment made by members of a particular society of apostolic life has a spiritual significance. For instance, when Saint Philip Neri founded his society of Oratorian priests and brothers in the sixteenth century, he declined to have them make any canonically binding commitment to the society because he wished each Oratorian priest and brother to have a sense of perfect freedom in the daily choice to live the Oratorian life. For this reason, although Oratorians do live in obedience to the Rule of the society, they do not profess vows. Instead Oratorians make a simple statement of their intention to persevere in their chosen way of life.

The Spirituality of Societies of Apostolic Life

Like religious communities, each society of apostolic life has its own founder, spirituality, and charism, so no two societies of apostolic life are exactly alike. One element of spirituality that is common to all societies of apostolic life, however,

Well-Known Societies of Apostolic Life

Here is a list of some of the better-known societies of apostolic life. How many sound familiar to you?

- **Oratorians of Saint Philip Neri:** Saint Philip Neri originally founded this society of priests in the sixteenth century to provide spiritual support and guidance to lay prayer groups. Today Oratorian priests live in independent local communities called Oratories. Each individual Oratory is free to choose its own primary apostolates, with the permission of the local diocesan bishop.

- **Daughters of Charity:** Founded by Saint Vincent de Paul and Saint Louise de Marillac in 1633, this society is dedicated to works of charity at the service of the poor.

- **Society of Saint Sulpice (Sulpicians):** Founded in the seventeenth century by Fr. Jean Jacques Olier, this society of diocesan priests is dedicated to priestly formation in seminaries.

- **Paulist Fathers:** This society of priests, founded in 1858 by Fr. Isaac Thomas Hecker, is dedicated to the apostolate of evangelization, especially through use of the media. Today the Paulists are known for their outreach to fallen-away Catholics and to young adults seeking to deepen their faith.

- **Maryknoll Missionary Fathers:** The Maryknoll Fathers are dedicated to foreign missionary work. The society was founded in 1910 by two priests, Fr. Thomas Price and Fr. James Walsh, and is famous for its missionary work in east Asia. Several Maryknoll priests are counted among the Church's martyrs.

- **Glenmary Home Missioners:** This society of priests, founded in 1939 by Fr. William Howard Bishop, carries out missionary work exclusively in the United States. Glenmary priests serve in areas of the United States where Catholics are in an extreme minority, often providing the Sacraments to American Catholics who would otherwise be unable to receive them due to geographical isolation.

- **Priestly Fraternity of Saint Peter:** This society was founded in 1988 to celebrate the liturgy according to the 1962 *Roman Missal* for those Catholics with a spiritual attachment to the older form of the Mass.

is a commitment to apostolic service. Like all consecrated people, members of societies of apostolic life are called first and foremost to an apostolate of prayer and witness. But societies of apostolic life place greater emphasis on their active apostolate than do most religious communities.

Societies of apostolic life are essentially communities of men or women called by God to a specific kind of apostolic work. For example, the Maryknoll Missionary Fathers have the foreign missions as a fundamental aspect of their vocation. Joining the Maryknoll Fathers is almost synonymous with a desire to spread the Gospel in foreign countries.

The apostolate of a society of apostolic life is a major source of its spirituality. Members of societies of apostolic life are especially committed to expressing their love of God through their apostolic mission. Likewise, they look to their apostolic work as an opportunity to grow closer to Christ and as a way to imitate him in his love for all people. ✝

Article 41 Secular Institutes

© hunta/Shutterstock.com

In the Gospel of Luke, Jesus preaches a brief but powerful parable: "To what shall I compare the kingdom of God? It is like yeast that a woman took and mixed [in] with three measures of wheat flour until the whole batch of dough was leavened" (13:20–21).

In this parable Jesus is telling us that although God's grace is often hidden and unseen, that does *not* mean that it cannot work wonders in the world! Even if a Christian does not appear unusual to the rest of the world, God can still use him or her to accomplish great things in advancing his Kingdom. The image of the Christian as leaven hidden in the world is central to the spirituality of secular institutes.

What Is a Secular Institute?

A secular institute is an organization for members of the faithful who feel called to live the evangelical counsels as completely as possible, while at the same time living fully in the world as laypeople.

moderators
Those who hold a place of authority within a secular institute; similar to the superior of a religious congregation.

A wide variety of secular institutes are active throughout the world. Like religious communities, each secular institute has its own charism, spirituality, and particular apostolic focus. Membership in a secular institute also demands a commitment to the evangelical counsels.

But unlike those in religious life, members of secular institutes usually do not live together in community or take on common apostolic projects (although some do in certain circumstances). Secular institute members typically live in their own homes, meeting with the other members of their institute on a regular basis so they can encourage and support one another in their mutual vocation. Members of secular institutes provide for themselves financially through their individual careers while also contributing to the material support of their institute.

All secular institute members promise to live a life of chaste celibacy. They observe the counsel of poverty through a commitment to a simple lifestyle, but they are able to own personal property. Secular institute members promise obedience to the rules and **moderators** of their institute in the ways defined in their constitutions.

The Mission of Secular Institutes

As part of the mission and spirituality of secular institutes, members focus on fully committing to Christ in order to bring the message of the Gospel to all areas of our culture, including the most secular. To accomplish this members of secular institutes consecrate themselves to God through the evangelical counsels while integrating fully into civic society.

Consecrated people with visible and public vocations often cannot evangelize the secular world from within, because the very fact of their public consecration obliges them to be set apart. Because of this secular institutes are unique among the various forms of consecrated life.

The vocation of secular institute members is to be witnesses in the world, bringing the Gospel into places and situations in which clergy and other consecrated persons ordinarily would not have the opportunity to minister and teach. For example, secular institute members are called to bring a Christian witness to the worlds of politics, public education, business and financial establishments, and the secular media.

History of Secular Institutes

Secular institutes are the newest form of consecrated life in the Church, having been formally recognized as a distinct vocation only in the mid-twentieth century. However, our modern secular institutes were anticipated in some ways by medieval and Renaissance-era lay fraternities. For example, in the fourteenth century, Saint Catherine of Siena joined a lay Dominican group called the Mantellate. These women—primarily widows—lived lives of chastity, prayer, penance, and service to the poor according to a specific rule of life but continued living in their own homes among their families.

Similarly, the Ursuline Order was originally intended by its foundress, Saint Angela Merici, to have a structure similar to that of a secular institute. Saint Angela's original vision for her "Company of Saint Ursula" involved a sisterhood of committed celibate laywomen dedicated to the mission of educating young girls. But because of Church law at the time, the early Ursulines were eventually required to become a more traditional religious order, adapting to the common practices of religious life, including some cloister regulations.

During the French Revolution, when established religious communities were often forcibly disbanded and new communities forbidden, Fr. Pierre Joseph de Clorivière, SJ, founded the Priests of the Heart of Jesus in 1791 to support diocesan clergy in the exercise of their ministry, often made arduous by the hostile cultural climate. Because the Priests of the Heart of Jesus were not technically a religious order, they could thrive when they would have otherwise been violently suppressed.

The late nineteenth century saw renewed interest in this form of consecrated life. Through the early twentieth century, groups of Catholics came together to form provisional associations for the support of those who wished to profess the evangelical counsels in the context of a lay life in society. However, none of these preliminary groups enjoyed full approval from the Church at first, for the simple reason that the Church lacked a category under which they could be approved.

Then in 1947 Pope Pius XII promulgated the apostolic constitution *Provida Mater Ecclesia (Provident Mother Church)*. This document officially established secular institutes as a new form of dedication in the life of the Church.

As a result some early groups of consecrated laypeople finally found their home in the Church, being formally approved as secular institutes. Today new secular institutes continue to be formed, and older ones continue to attract new members. ✝

Saint Catherine of Siena

Catherine was born in 1347, in Siena, Italy, the twenty-fourth child born to her parents. Having experienced visions of Christ as a young child, she dedicated her life and her virginity to Christ, but her family pressured her to marry and tried to discourage her vocational call. Catherine protested by fasting, seeking solitude, and even cutting off her hair. She later wrote that God had shown her how to retreat to a "secret cell," a place inside her soul where she could find comfort and learn to see Jesus, the Blessed Virgin Mary, and the Apostles in her family members.

Her family finally relented and gave her permission to live as she wished. She lived as a hermit in a small room in her father's house for a time and became a Dominican tertiary, a lay member of the Dominican order who did not take religious vows or live inside the convent. She also experienced the stigmata—bodily marks or sensations of pain corresponding with the Crucifixion wounds of Christ. Then, in response to another vision, her dedication to the Church took on a public dimension. She traveled widely to serve people who were poor, sick, or imprisoned. She worked to end civil wars in her country and helped to encourage Pope Gregory XI to end the Avignon Papacy and return to Rome from France.

In 1380 Catherine collapsed after a stroke and died at the age of thirty-three. Catherine is especially known for her writings on the spiritual life and her influence on European politics as well as on the Church. She was canonized a saint and was the first layperson named a Doctor of the Church. Saint Catherine's feast day is celebrated on April 29.

Part Review

1. Write a short outline of the history of consecrated life. Be sure to include the five major forms of consecrated life recognized by the Church today.

2. Briefly describe the spirituality of consecrated virgins.

3. How are hermits called to serve the Church?

4. Compare and contrast religious communities with societies of apostolic life.

5. In what ways are secular institutes unique among the various forms of consecrated life?

6. What form of consecrated life do you find to be most interesting, and why? What questions do you still have about this form of consecrated life?

Discerning God's Will

Part 1

Discernment: A Conversation with God

Learning about vocations can be an academic exercise. There are such rich historical and theological understandings behind each of the vocational states of life that there is, indeed, much to learn. But now that you have explored the meaning of the different states of life, how do you go about the process of discovering which one God is calling you to live?

In this part you will be led from the theoretical to the practical. By focusing on a process called discernment, you will be introduced to the skills and practices essential to discovering God's will for you—skills and practices you can use throughout your life but especially when you are seeking to discover your vocation.

God wants to fulfill our heart's desire for happiness, which is found only in communion with him. Part of fulfilling this desire for communion with God is discerning and living out your Christian vocation. This part will introduce you to the tools to begin to do just that.

The articles in this part address the following topics:

^{Article}**42** Where Is God Leading Me?

discernment

From a Latin word meaning "to separate or to distinguish between," it is the practice of listening for God's call in our lives and distinguishing between good and bad choices.

Things looked bleak for the People of God exiled in Babylon. But the Prophet Jeremiah had heard God's Word, and he wrote a letter to the exiles, encouraging them to keep faith with God, to trust him with their lives and their futures:

> For I know well the plans I have in mind for you . . . plans for your welfare and not for woe, so as to give you a future of hope. When you call me, and come and pray to me, I will listen to you. When you look for me, you will find me. Yes, when you seek me with all your heart, I will let you find me . . . and I will change your lot. (Jeremiah 29:11–14).

We know that Scripture was not written for only the people of the past; it was also written for us, here in the present. Sacred Scripture was written so we might hear the Word of God and receive the hope and encouragement we need to lives as Christians. But, in order to truly hear God's Word and find hope and encouragement to live according to God's will, we need to trust God.

You may feel that you do not know God well enough to trust him with *today*, let alone your entire future. But, if that is the case, take it as a sign to trust him even more—to make a "leap of faith" into the depths of God's love. Start a conversation with God. Share all your fears and hopes with him. (He knows them already, but sharing our fears and hopes with God is in itself an act of trust.) Take Jeremiah's words to heart and find more words in Scripture that give you courage. When you can begin to trust God with your life and your future—even if your trust, or faith, is the size of a mustard seed (see Matthew 17:20, Luke 17:6)—you can begin a process of **discernment**, the process of finding God's will.

Taking time for self-reflection is an important tool for growing in holiness and discovering one's vocation. When and where do you take time to reflect?

© Isaac Koval/iStockphoto.com

The Call to Marriage

Often the advice of family and friends helps the discernment process. Through open communication we gain understanding of our situation in ways we could not see ourselves. This was the case with Matt Rivera. Let's let him tell his story:

I was dating Molly, a girl from my hometown, all through college. She was easy to be with, and she made even ordinary things we did together—like babysitting her cousins or walking through a museum—fun and interesting. Anyway, the summer after we graduated from college, her family decided to leave town, and she was going to move with them. I was really kind of at a loss.

When I told my sister the news, she asked, "Matt, how do you feel about that?"

"Rotten," I said. "I don't want her to leave. She is my best friend, and I really love her. I can't image her not being a part of my everyday life."

"Well," she said, "Sounds like you may have met your future wife. Perhaps you should ask her to marry you."

You could have knocked me over with a feather. Marriage? A month ago I was a college kid and now—marriage? Yet, on the other hand, I couldn't imagine life without Molly. I realized that my life had come to revolve around hers.

So after some more time, I did it. I asked Molly to marry me. And she said yes! Marriage has helped Molly and me to continue to grow together. We discuss everything, and if we disagree, we don't make a decision right away. We have a three-day rule to give us time to talk about something and find a compromise we both can live with.

And my sister? She entered a convent and now teaches in a school. I call her Sister Ann Landers because she listened to me and gave me such good advice!

contemplation
A form of wordless prayer in which one is fully focused on the presence of God; sometimes defined as "resting in God."

meditation
A form of prayer involving a variety of methods and techniques, in which one engages the mind, imagination, and emotions to focus on a particular truth, biblical theme, or other spiritual matter.

The process of discernment is a process of conversation with God. Sometimes that conversation takes place quietly between you and God. Sometimes it includes a wise and knowledgeable person, such as a priest, teacher, or counselor. The conversation may emerge during Mass, while helping someone who needs you at that moment, while reading Scripture, or while reflecting on your day. You may be surprised when the conversation with God continues in the midst of a school day, on a camping trip, or when hanging out with friends. But you really should not be surprised. God is always with you, and you are asking him very important questions: What is my vocation in life? Where are you leading me? These are questions God has been waiting all your life to help you to answer! ✝

Live It!

A Discernment Checklist

Here is a short checklist to use as a reminder of all the ways you can discern the desires of your heart in conversation with God:

- pray daily, using one or more of the three major expressions of Christian prayer: **contemplation**, **meditation**, and **vocal prayer**
- participate in the Eucharist each Sunday (or Saturday evening), on Holy Days of Obligation, and on other weekdays when possible
- receive the Sacrament of Penance and Reconciliation
- participate in Eucharistic devotions and Marian devotions
- talk with a priest, campus minister, or other qualified spiritual director
- seek advice from family and friends
- read accounts of saints' lives, paying particular attention to how they discerned and followed God's will
- learn more about the Church's teachings
- read Sacred Scripture

Copy this list into your journal or on a sheet of paper to remind yourself of all of the actions that can support your discernment.

Article 43 God Sees the Heart

In the Gospel of Matthew, Jesus says to us: "Come to me
. . . and I will give you rest. Take my yoke upon you and
learn from me . . . and you will find rest for yourselves. For
my yoke is easy, and my burden light" (11:28–30).

Who says this to us? Who is this Jesus? He is the Christ,
the Anointed One, the only Son of God. True God and true
man, he came into the world in flesh like ours, sent by the
Father and the Holy Spirit, to be our Brother, Friend, and
Savior. Whatever our Christian call may be, he asks us to follow him and assures us that if we do, we will find rest—not
physical rest, but spiritual rest. We might call it peace.

In the process of discerning God's will, it is good to
remember the mystery of the Holy Trinity, the central mystery of the Christian faith and life. This is the mystery of one God in three Divine Persons: Father,
Son, and Holy Spirit. As the three Persons in one
God worked together to create and then to save the
world, so they work together in our lives to bring us
to the truth of our call. As you continue to discern
God's will in your life, remember that God is with
you. Incorporated into Christ at Baptism, you have
God as your Father, who wants only good for you.
You are guided, if you ask, by the Holy Spirit, who,
even without words, prays within you. Through the
gift of grace, we move toward the goal of Christian
life, union with the Holy Trinity in Heaven.

It is also good to remember that God's will is a
loving will. God cannot will evil. Evil exists because
we human beings choose it, and God gave us that
choice when he gave us free will. God can invite,
urge, and entreat, but he will never force his will
upon us.

vocal prayer

A prayer that is spo-
ken aloud or silently,
such as the Lord's
Prayer.

providence

The guidance, mate-
rial goods, and care
provided by God that
is sufficient to meet
our needs.

© PavleMarjanovic/Shutterstock.com

God's Loving Will in Your Life

God already has, in a way, stacked the deck toward the truth
of your call. In your life circumstances allowed by God's
providence; in your own gifts and talents; in the good desires
that he has sown in your heart; in the guidance of Scripture,

Christ assures us
that if we follow him,
we will have peace.
Christ is an integral
part of our discern-
ment process, along
with the Father and
the Holy Spirit.

A Vocation to the Priesthood

Let's let Father Jerry, a parish priest, tell his discernment story:

I went to a Catholic grade school and high school. I was an altar server but otherwise kind of on the fringes of parish life, as kids often are. Sometimes one or another of the priests would suggest to us that we consider the priesthood as a life choice, but those suggestions kind of rolled off my back. I was in community college near the middle of my sophomore year when I realized that I wanted to go on for a full degree. I had to choose a transfer school, a school that would lead me to a bachelor's degree. So I began looking at schools, talking to people and looking online at various places. Then this little nudge, I guess you could call it, came up in my mind. "Be a priest," it said. "Be a priest."

I was taken aback. This thought seemed to come from deep within me, yet it had an authority that I could not ignore. I went to my parish priest and told him that I was thinking of the priesthood. We talked a few times, and I realized that basically I had always cared about people and that God had always been a part of my life. Then he took me to visit the diocesan seminary. It was a big building, but I felt at home there, strangely enough. I met some of the guys who were studying there, and it just seemed like the right place and the right next step.

I'm a parish priest now. I realized a few years ago that my life would be shaped by God through a parish full of people and that I was privileged to help bring God and people together. I'm busy, peaceful, and happy. What more could I ask for?

© Bill Wittman/www.wpwittman.com

Tradition, and the Church's Magisterium (the Church's living teaching office), he has given you hints of his call to you.

In your discernment, it might be helpful for you to recognize what God has already done for you, what gifts he has already given to you. Consider the Church, enhancing your awareness of God's presence in your life through so many ways, especially through Scripture, Tradition, and the Sacraments, day after day and year after year. Consider your family, your school, your teachers, your opportunities for service, and your vacation times. Consider the beauty of the earth. Consider the wonder of animals and plants. And consider all the things about you—your special gifts and talents, your unique self, everything that makes you *you*: it all comes from God. Your discernment process will lead you to ask questions like these: What shall I do with all these gifts? How will I use them? How do they relate to the state of life God may be calling me to? How will I contribute to the world? How will I give back to the Lord all that he has given to me? ✝

Pray It!

Lord, What Do You Want Me to Do?

Through meditation we can discover the stirrings of our hearts and gain insight about what God wants us to do. There are many ways to meditate, but here are some simple steps for getting started:

1. Select a focus for your meditation, such as a Scripture passage, a spiritual writing, or an event from the life of Christ.
2. Choose a quiet place that is as free from distraction as possible.
3. Begin by assuming a posture conducive to prayer, such as kneeling or sitting.
4. Recall that you are in the holy presence of God and ask for his help in understanding his will for your life.
5. Turn your attention to the selected focus of your meditation, allowing it to engage your thoughts, imagination, and emotions. For example, if you are meditating on an event in the life of Christ, try to imagine yourself in the event.
6. Conclude with a prayer of thanksgiving.

Article 44 Listening to God

Our culture is in perpetual surround-sound. Think about all the different sounds you hear during a typical day. Besides the typical sounds in our industrial and mechanical society (traffic, trains, jet engines, and so on), we have electronic sounds that are even closer to us: television, radio, cell phones, various personal listening devices, and computers equipped with all sorts of sound-carrying features. And then, of course, we do hear some of the same sounds our ancestors heard: the twitter of birds, the honk of geese, the wind in the trees.

All these sounds can make it difficult for us to be comfortable in silence and solitude. We may find it hard, even when alone, to dwell peacefully without a wall of sound separating ourselves from our deepest thoughts and desires.

In the discernment process, it is important to carve out times of quiet listening into your day and week. Start with 10 minutes a day, maybe in a nearby church, library, or other quiet place. Give those 10 minutes to God. Say what the young Samuel said as he did the same thing millennia ago, "Speak, LORD, for your servant is listening" (1 Samuel 3:9). As you try this for a few days, you may think you are wasting time, because nothing may seem to be happening. But beneath the surface and in your heart, you are creating a space of clarity and openness toward God. And because of this, you will be better able to discern, during the rest of your day, what God may be saying to you through the people and circumstances of your life. These 10 minutes will plant the seeds of peace in your heart so that you will recognize the path of peace when it opens to you.

What sounds, voices, and other distractions are competing for your attention on a daily basis? What can you do to create some quiet reflection time each day?

© wavebreakmedia ltd/Shutterstock.com

Gradually words, symbols, events, and images that you meet through Sacred Scripture and Sacred Tradition and in your everyday life will come to have meaning because your quiet time has helped you to become more open to them. If you are open to God "speaking" through these words, symbols,

A Vocation to a Brother's Life

Often the circumstances of our lives, even unhappy circumstances, point us in a direction and help us to discern a vocation. As an example, let us listen to the story of Brother Anthony:

> I found my vocation in high school. I was the eldest in my family, with four younger brothers and sisters. We had problems at home, and, as the eldest, I had a lot of responsibility at home with the younger children. In my sophomore year, these problems and responsibilities were affecting my life at school. My grades began to slip. and I was having a hard time. So I talked to a counselor—who was a religious brother, a teaching brother—to get some help.
>
> That took a lot of courage—to let someone know my family problems. But he really did help me. All the brothers did. And I wasn't anything special. I wasn't a big athlete or a particularly great student. I was just an average kid. And they looked out for me. And I began to want to help other kids the way I had been helped.

Anthony joined the brothers who taught at his high school and became a high school teacher himself. He is now a professor at a Catholic college sponsored by his religious community.

events, and images (and with the counsel of a trusted and qualified spiritual director), you will be led.

In all prayer we tend to want answers rather quickly. But try to give it time. Sometimes answers do come quickly, but often discerning a path in life takes a while.

Other Important Things to Do

Attending Mass regularly will help you to discern God's call. Take advantage of the richness of the Eucharist—in the proclamation of Sacred Scripture, in the liturgical prayers, and especially in the Body and Blood of Christ. Jesus wants to be food for your journey, to strengthen you and to show you his love.

The other Sacraments will help and strengthen you too, especially the Sacrament of Penance and Reconciliation. We need only look at the lives of many saints to realize that they were not always perfect. They became holy because they were willing to change what they could in order to do God's work of love in the world. Experiencing the forgiveness of God and receiving sacramental grace in the Sacrament of Penance and Reconciliation will strengthen your relation-ship with him and will help you to live your call to Christian discipleship.

Having a spiritual director or advisor is helpful. Talk-ing things over with someone experienced in helping others

Catholic Wisdom

Suscipe (Prayer of Surrender)

This prayer was composed by Saint Ignatius Loyola.

Take, Lord, and receive all my liberty,
my memory, my understanding,
and my entire will,
all I have and call my own.

You have given all to me.
To you, Lord, I return it.

Everything is yours; do with it what you will.
Give me only your love and your grace,
that is enough for me.

to discern God's call, such as a pastor or a parish priest, can provide spiritual guidance and practical insight. Talking things over with family and trusted friends who know you well and are supportive can be helpful too. ✝

Part Review

1. What is discernment?

2. What role does God's providence take in our lives and in our discernment of his call?

3. What is the value of spending time each day in silence with God?

4. Explain how the Eucharist can help in the discernment process.

5. Describe the role of the Sacrament of Penance and Reconciliation in the discernment process.

6. How can a spiritual counselor or a spiritual director help in the discernment process?

Part 2

Walking with God

As the Prophet Micah proclaims, we are called to "walk humbly" with God (see Micah 6:8). But the process of discernment is a particular walk with a particular focus. In this part we take a closer look at this decision-making process, keeping in mind that even after one has chosen a vocation in life with the help of God, other important decisions need to be made throughout life.

So even though you may feel that this information is not relevant to you now—perhaps you already have a clear sense of the vocational state of life God is calling you to—you may need this information later. Making important decisions involves our whole self—spiritual, intellectual, and emotional—and in this part we learn how self-knowledge and a sincere desire to know God's will can help us, now or at any time, throughout our lives.

In this part we will gain a deeper awareness of the presence of God in our lives by recalling the very significant event of Pentecost. Through the Holy Spirit, Jesus is with us always, and in the Holy Spirit we too are called to bring the love of Christ to all the world.

The articles in this part address the following topics:

- Article 45: Here I Am, Lord (page 199)
- Article 46: Set the Whole World on Fire! (page 203)

45 Here I Am, Lord

Above all, the process of discernment is a search for truth—
the truth of your own being in relationship to God and his
will for your life. This process involves prayer, of course, as
we have already discussed, but it also involves a search for
self-knowledge. Increasing your self-knowledge will help you
in the process of discerning the state of life God calls you to.

You already have a certain amount of self-knowledge.
Learning about yourself—your needs, desires, prefer-
ences, gifts, talents, and weaknesses—is an inevitable part
of growing up. You may have been fortunate to have found
someone with whom you can be honest and truthful about
your strengths and weaknesses, and that person may have

We often find out
who we are through
relationships with
other people. Who in
your life helps you
to understand more
about yourself?

Catholic Wisdom

A Word from Pope Benedict XVI

In his homily at World Youth Day in 2011, Pope Benedict XVI encouraged young
people to answer the question Jesus asked of his Apostles, "Who do you say that I
am?" (Mark 8:29):

> Say to him: "Jesus, I know that you are the Son of God, who have given your life for
> me. I want to follow you faithfully and to be led by your word. You know me and you
> love me. I place my trust in you and I put my whole life into your hands. I want you to
> be the power that strengthens me and the joy which never leaves me." ("Apostolic
> Journey to Madrid on the Occasion of the 26th World Youth Day, August 18,
> 2011")

helped you to understand and work with those strengths and weaknesses so far. We all must make efforts to work with our particular gifts and limitations, for our own sake as well as for the sake of others.

The discernment process invites you to make an intentional effort to find out who you are. You may want to put together, just for your own information, a "profile" of yourself, including things like talents, hobbies, likes, dislikes, and areas needing improvement. Sometimes seeing a summary of yourself on paper gives you a more objective viewpoint on this person you call "me." It is truly amazing to think that by finding out the truth about yourself, you can also find the seeds of your vocation and a clearer sense of the state of life you are called to.

In this search for truth, the tools of modern psychology can be helpful. Your counselors at school may offer various personality inventories or other instruments of self-knowledge. These vary in accuracy and intention, so they should be interpreted only with professional help, but sometimes they can pinpoint areas of possible interest and growth that you may have overlooked simply because you have never been exposed to these possibilities. They may also highlight areas of your life you need to work on to make them truly helpful to you. Whatever you think your vocational state in life may be, knowing yourself and how to help yourself grow will be an asset.

Seeking God's Will

Another part of the truth is seeking God's will. In this we have no greater model than Jesus himself, who, as the Son of God, followed his Father's will perfectly. This does not mean that he followed the Father's will without sacrifice and suffering. Even a cursory reading of the Gospels convinces us that Jesus' earthly life was not free of difficulty. The Epistle to the Hebrews explores this mystery. The writer of this epistle puts the words of Psalm 7 into the mouth of Jesus at the moment of the Incarnation:

> When he came into the world, he said:
> "Sacrifice and offering you did not desire,
>   but a body you prepared for me;
> holocausts and sin offerings you took no delight in.

Then I said, 'As is written of me in the scroll,
    Behold, I come to do your will, O God.'"

(10:5–7)

The Word of God became flesh and was always fully open to the will of the Father. We too, by God's gracious plan, have been given life on earth so that we might be instruments of peace and love in the world. Our attitude toward the discovery of God's will for us should be one of openmindedness,

The Vocation to the Committed Single Life

It is true that many people experience single life as a temporary or transitional state. However, when someone feels called to commit to celibate single life as a permanent gift to God and neighbor, this commitment may be considered a vocational state of life. Sarah's story might provide some insight into how somebody can come to understand this particular calling:

Ever since I was younger, I knew that I was called to help others. Of course, we are all called to reach out to those in need, but I felt I was supposed to do this as my life's main focus. Not only am I a social worker in the inner city, but I also teach adult education classes on weeknights and serve as a founding member of a new homeless shelter in the community.

People ask me if I ever get exhausted, and I certainly do at times. But I am also filled with life, doing what I love and knowing that I am using my gifts and talents in the way God intended me to. As you might imagine, this doesn't leave much time for the possibility of marriage and family life, but I am okay with that. I get so much joy from my work within this community and the incredible people that surround me that I know I am called to remain single as my permanent vocation. It certainly isn't everybody's vocation, but it is how I feel I can best live the way God is calling me to live.

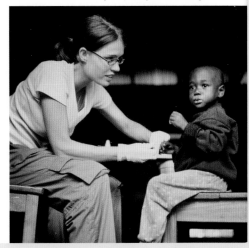

© Mika/Corbis

intellect

The divine gift that gives us the ability to see and understand the order of things that God places within creation and to know and understand God through the created order.

free will

The gift from God that allows human beings to choose from among various actions, for which we are held accountable. It is the basis for moral responsibility.

faith, trust, eagerness, and joy. God wills only good for us, and the process of discernment can help us to find the truth and live it in our lives.

Choosing the Wrong Vocation

Is it possible to choose the wrong vocation? Theoretically, yes. We are fallible human beings, and even with the best of intentions and the best of counsel, we may make a mistake. This is why we are urged to spend time learning about and praying about a life choice before we make a commitment to it. Most religious orders allow several years for this process. The priesthood and the diaconate also require years of learning and discernment. Young people considering marriage are urged to take time to learn not only about themselves but also about their potential spouses through premarital programs offered by their parishes or dioceses.

Saying No to God

Is it possible to say no to God about a particular vocation we feel called to? Yes, it is possible. We have been given the gifts of **intellect** and **free will**. We have the freedom to shape our own lives, but we are called to use our intellect to discern what is good and then to freely choose the good. But we need to keep in mind that if we feel that God is truly calling us to a particular vocation, saying no to God is also saying no to ourselves and our deepest desire for communion with him. This is no small thing. It is no small thing because each one of us has only one life. Saying no to the vocation to which God calls us means saying no to his gift of grace. When we reject God's grace, we make our journey to eternal life more difficult. Rejecting God's call to serve him in a particular vocation may even jeopardize our eternal salvation—communion with God in Heaven.

When one is young, it may seem like there is plenty of time ahead to figure out and respond to God's call regarding a particular vocation. But try to imagine how someone would feel if, after thirty or forty years, he or she admitted: "I could have been a priest, but I was afraid to talk to anyone about it"; "I could have been a sister, but all my friends were talking about living away on their own at college, and I didn't want to miss out on what they all shared"; "I could have married, but I didn't want to give up my freedom to worry just about myself." A serious discernment process can uncover the truth, dissolve fears, and pave the way to a future without regrets.

That is not to say that discerning and committing to a vocational call is easy. Even the great Saint Paul had this problem of resistance to God's will early in his life. He blocked it out and continued to persecute the followers of Jesus. Finally Jesus appeared to him on the way to one of his raids against Christians and said, "Saul, Saul, why are you persecuting me?" (Acts of the Apostles 9:4). This encounter with Jesus led Paul to his new life as an Apostle and as one of the most important leaders in the early Church.

The same is true of us. Even if we somehow "miss" our true calling in life, God will be merciful and loving and will not deny us happiness or joy and will welcome us when we finally accept his call and respond. And when we feel apprehensive about the vocation to which we hear God calling us, it can help to remember that he gives us the grace we need to live out the commitments and responsibilities of his call. But until we accept and respond to his call, we may experience something like the feeling we have when we are wearing clothes that don't quite fit: something is too tight here, or falling loose there, and we are uncomfortable. We may feel like we are not living to our full potential. Making an effort in adolescence and early adulthood to discern how best to use the gifts God has given us and in which state of life can help us to find true happiness and holiness in this life and set us on the path to eternal life with God. ✝

© Arnold John Labrentz/Shutterstock.com

Article 46 Set the Whole World on Fire!

At the right place and at the right time, fire can be a positive force of nature. Wildfires are sometimes necessary for nature to renew itself, and, as frightening as these fires can be, they are often left to burn unimpeded unless they threaten lives and property. Wildfires in nature burn up dead wood and choking underbrush so that the sun can reach straight down into the forest and encourage new growth.

Fire: A Symbol of the Presence of God

These facts help us to understand the symbolism of fire as it appears in both the Old and the New Testaments. In the Book of Exodus, God revealed himself to Moses through the burning bush—a bush enveloped in flames but not consumed. As Moses approached this curious phenomenon, God called him by name: "Moses! Moses!" (Exodus 3:4). Then God said: "Do not come near! Remove your sandals from your feet, for the place where you stand is holy ground" (3:5). God continued, "I am the God of your father . . . the God of Abraham, the God of Isaac, and the God of Jacob" (3:6). In this event fire is the sign of the presence of God, and with this sign began the journey of God's people from the slavery of Egypt to the freedom of the Promised Land.

The Prophet Jeremiah experienced the prophetic Word of God within him as a fire that he could not extinguish:

> I say I will not mention him,
>> I will no longer speak in his name.
> But then it is as if fire is burning in my heart,
>> imprisoned in my bones;
> I grow weary holding back,
>> I cannot!
>
> (Jeremiah 20:9)

Jesus used the symbolism of fire when he was teaching the crowds: "I have come to set the earth on fire, and how I wish it were already blazing! There is a baptism with which I must be baptized, and how great is my anguish until it is accomplished!" (Luke 12:49–50). If fire is a symbol for the presence of God in the hearts and minds of people, then surely Jesus meant that he wanted everyone in the world to know God. But first the earth must be purified in order that the new growth, growth in the Holy Spirit, would emerge. Jesus himself would bring this about through his Passion, death on the Cross, Resurrection, and Ascension. Then the fire of the Holy Spirit could descend into the world and set hearts and minds on fire with love for God.

A Call to Religious Life

Looking to the lives of others is one way of discerning a vocation. Who are your role models? What do they do? How do they do it? Would you like to be like them? Let's listen to Sister Gina as she explains how her role models helped her to discern her vocation:

> The sisters in my community taught me both in high school and in college, and, to me, they were the meaning of religious life. Whenever I thought about "life after college," the idea of religious life would come up. Even when I tried not to think about it, I would find myself thinking about it, so I decided to pursue the idea and see where it led. I had to be honest with my own life.
>
> Talking with the sisters and others led to entrance into the community. I was a music major in college and was able to pursue that interest in the community. I have taught music in high school and have been a music minister in parishes. But, as one of the sisters told me early on, "You're going to be using talents you never knew you had!" and that's been true. Community life has brought out the best in me, I would say.
>
> One of the best parts of community life is the shared mission. We help one another to do our best for God and for the people we serve. And another part is the shared fun. There is always something to look forward to—a special feast day, family visits, even days when we work hard cleaning all day and end with a pizza party. The support of a community prayer life is central to me. I really thank God every day for bringing me to community. I always say that I got more than I bargained for!

The Day of Pentecost

The day of Pentecost (fifty days after Passover) was a day of festival for the Jews. They gathered in Jerusalem to thank God for the firstfruits of the harvest. On this very day, the Apostles and Mary were gathered together in prayer in the Upper Room in Jerusalem, for Jesus had told them to wait for "the promise of the Father about which you have heard me speak; for John baptized with water, but in a few days you will be baptized with the holy Spirit" (Acts of the Apostles 1:4–5).

And what a Baptism that was! A strong wind filled the house. There were tongues of fire over the heads of each one. And suddenly the Apostles were given the ability to witness in different tongues. It was a spectacular beginning.

The Fire in Our Lives

The world continues to be in need of an awareness of the fire that is God's presence. This is the kind of fire that is generated by those who have a passion for God and for his people and who witness to his presence through their words and actions—through their very lives.

Live It!

Walking in Footsteps

We walk in the footsteps of the saints, and we walk in the footsteps of those who have gone before us. To learn more about those who have accepted God's challenge to live according to his call, follow these steps:

1. Read a biography of a saint. (Ask your teacher for suggestions.) How did this saint discover his or her vocation? How did the saint live out his or her call? What lessons can you learn from this saint?
2. Talk to a married person, a vowed religious, a priest, and a faithful single person. Ask each one to tell you the story of her or his call. Share these stories with your classmates, noting what you learned.
3. Begin a daily journal and promise to keep it for one month. Focus on one question: What is God asking of me? After two weeks, if you feel moved to do so, share your journal with a trusted adult, counselor, or spiritual director. Finally, at the end of the month, write down what you learned from keeping your journal.

By our baptismal call, we are commissioned to set the world on fire by witnessing to, and helping others to recognize, the presence of God's love. How we do that best is by discovering God's will for our own lives in each moment and by living that out fully in the vocation to which we have been called.

Through your study of the different vocational states of life presented in this text and a commitment to entering the process of discernment, you are continuing to fully become who God created you to be. In this way you will discover your own call to a particular vocation and, in so doing, will find the state of life in which you can most effectively ignite the world with the Good News.

A generous response to God's invitation to love and to serve him in a particular vocational state of life can truly be a "Pentecost moment" in your life, when through the power of the Holy Spirit you will be able to witness to God's love, and in ways you never thought possible. By walking in your own truth in the vocation you are called to, you will fulfill Saint Catherine of Siena's challenge to her followers and to us today: "Be who God meant you to be and you will set the whole world on fire!" ✝

Pray It!

A Meditation by Cardinal Newman

This prayer by Cardinal John Henry Newman (1801–1890) reflects how each of us is uniquely called to serve God. As you read it, you might consider writing your own prayer that you could use as you reflect upon your vocation.

God has created me to do him some definite service; he has committed some work to me which he has not committed to another. I have my mission. . . . I am a link in a chain, a bond of connection between persons. He has not created me for naught. I shall do good, I shall do his work; I shall be an angel of peace, a preacher of truth in my own place, while not intending it, if I do but keep his commandments and serve him in my calling.

Part Review

1. Why is finding out "who you are" important to the discernment process?

2. Who and what can help us to discover our strengths, weaknesses, abilities, and potential?

3. What should be our attitude in seeking God's will?

4. What does the symbol of fire mean in both the Old and New Testaments?

5. How does the "fire of the Holy Spirit" show itself in our lives?

6. What do you think it might mean for you to "set the world on fire"?

Glossary

A

abortion The deliberate termination of a pregnancy by killing the unborn child. It is a grave sin and a crime against human life. *(page 93)*

age of reason The age at which a person can be morally responsible. This is generally regarded to be the age of seven. *(page 23)*

annulment The declaration by the Church that a marriage is null and void, that is, it never existed as a sacramental union. Catholics who divorce must have the marriage annulled by the Church to be free to marry once again in the Church. *(page 90)*

apostolate The Christian person's activity that fulfills the apostolic nature of the whole Church when he or she works to extend the Kingdom of Christ to the entire world. If your school shares the wisdom of its founder, its namesake, or the charism of the religious order that founded it, it is important to learn about this person or order and his or her charism, because as a graduate you will likely want to incorporate this charism into your own apostolate. *(page 42)*

Apostolic Succession The uninterrupted passing on of apostolic preaching and authority from the Apostles directly to all bishops. It is accomplished through the laying on of hands when a bishop is ordained in the Sacrament of Holy Orders as instituted by Christ. The office of bishop is permanent, because at ordination a bishop is marked with an indelible, sacred character. *(page 117)*

ascetic Pertaining to spiritual discipline in which a person leads a strict life of simplicity and self-denial. *(page 171)*

atonement Reparation for wrongdoing or sin and reconciliation with God, accomplished for humankind by Christ's sacrifice. *(page 106)*

B

Beatitudes The teachings of Jesus during the Sermon on the Mount in which he describes the actions and attitudes that should characterize Christians and by which one can discover genuine meaning and happiness. *(page 13)*

breviary A prayer book that contains the prayers for the Liturgy of the Hours. *(page 169)*

C

cenobitic Monastic life lived in community rather than in solitude. *(page 173)*

charism A special gift or grace of the Holy Spirit given to an individual Christian or community, commonly for the benefit and building up of the entire Church. *(page 154)*

chastity The virtue by which people are able to successfully and healthfully integrate their sexuality into their total person; recognized as one of the fruits of the Holy Spirit. *(page 71)*

college of bishops The assembly of bishops, headed by the Pope, that holds the teaching authority and responsibility in the Church. *(page 117)*

consecrated life A state of life recognized by the Church in which a person publicly professes vows of poverty, chastity, and obedience. *(page 147)*

contemplation A form of wordless prayer in which one is fully focused on the presence of God; sometimes defined as "resting in God." *(page 190)*

contraception The deliberate attempt to interfere with the creation of new life as a result of sexual intercourse. It is morally wrong because a married couple must remain open to procreation whenever they engage in sexual intercourse. *(page 92)*

convalidation A wedding ceremony in which a man and a woman in a civil marriage have their marital union recognized and blessed by the Church. *(page 82)*

corporal works of mercy Charitable actions that respond to people's physical needs and show respect for human dignity. The traditional list of seven works includes feeding the hungry, giving drink to the thirsty, clothing the naked, sheltering the homeless, visiting the sick, visiting prisoners, and burying the dead. *(page 162)*

Counter-Reformation A movement of internal reform within the Church during the later sixteenth and early seventeenth centuries that came about as a response to the Protestant Reformation. *(page 176)*

covenant A personal, solemn promise of faithful love that involves mutual commitments and creates a sacred relationship. *(page 60)*

D

dalmatic The liturgical vestment proper to a deacon. A dalmatic is shaped like a large, loose tunic with sleeves. *(page 137)*

diaconate The vocation and ministry of a deacon. *(page 125)*

diocese Also known as a "particular" or "local" Church, the regional community of believers, who commonly gather in parishes, under the leadership of a bishop. At times, a diocese is determined not on the basis of geography but on the basis of language or rite. *(page 117)*

discernment From a Latin word meaning "to separate or to distinguish between," it is the practice of listening for God's call in our lives and distinguishing between good and bad choices. *(page 188)*

disparity of cult A marriage between a baptized Catholic and a nonbaptized person. *(page 77)*

dispensation Special permission to depart from the usual requirements in a given circumstance. *(page 75)*

E
episcopate The position or office of a bishop. *(page 117)*
eremitic Relating to the life of a hermit, characterized by self-denial and solitude. *(page 171)*
eschatological Having to do with the last things: the Last Judgment, the particular judgment, the resurrection of the body, Heaven, Hell, and Purgatory. *(page 155)*
evangelical counsels The call to go beyond the minimum rules of life required by God (such as the Ten Commandments and the precepts of the Church) and strive for spiritual perfection through a life marked by a commitment to chastity, poverty, and obedience. *(page 149)*
evangelize The action of proclaiming the Good News of Jesus Christ through words and witness. *(page 43)*

F
family of origin The family in which one was raised as a child. Families of origin can include parents, siblings, extended family members, or others who played a significant role in one's childhood and youth. *(page 67)*
free will The gift from God that allows human beings to choose from among various actions, for which we are held accountable. It is the basis for moral responsibility. *(page 202)*

H
Holy See This term is a translation of the Latin *sancta sedes*, which literally means "holy seat." The word *see* refers to a diocese or seat of a bishop. The Holy See is the seat of the central administration of the whole Church, under the leadership of the Pope, the Bishop of Rome. *(page 140)*

I
idolatry The worship of false gods in violation of the First Commandment. *(page 59)*
incardinated Placed under the authority of a particular bishop or the superior of a religious community. *(page 121)*
insignia Signs and symbols of one's office, ministry, or vocation. *(page 140)*
intellect The divine gift that gives us the ability to see and understand the order of things that God places within creation and to know and understand God through the created order. *(page 202)*

in vitro fertilization The fertilization of a woman's ovum (egg) with a man's sperm outside her body. The fertilized egg is transferred to the woman's uterus. The Church considers the process to be a moral violation of the dignity of procreation. *(page 94)*

L

laity (the lay faithful, laypeople) All members of the Church with the exception of those who are ordained as bishops, priests, or deacons. The laity share in Christ's role as priest, prophet, and king, witnessing to God's love and power in the world. *(page 40)*

lectio divina A Latin term meaning "divine reading." *Lectio divina* is a form of meditative prayer focused on a Scripture passage. It involves repetitive readings and periods of reflection and can serve as either private or communal prayer. *(page 172)*

Liturgy of the Hours Also known as the Divine Office, the official, public, daily prayer of the Catholic Church. The Divine Office provides standard prayers, Scripture readings, and reflections at regular hours throughout the day. *(page 122)*

M

Magisterium The Church's living teaching office, which consists of all bishops, in communion with the Pope, the Bishop of Rome. *(page 111)*

meditation A form of prayer involving a variety of methods and techniques, in which one engages the mind, imagination, and emotions to focus on a particular truth, biblical theme, or other spiritual matter. *(page 190)*

mendicant From a Latin root *mendicare*, meaning "to beg." Members of mendicant orders rely on charity for their support. *(page 175)*

mixed marriage A marriage between a Catholic and a baptized non-Catholic. *(page 77)*

moderators Those who hold a place of authority within a secular institute; similar to the superior of a religious congregation. *(page 182)*

N

natural family planning A morally acceptable way to time pregnancies based on the observation of a woman's naturally occurring times of fertility and infertility. *(page 76)*

natural law The moral law that can be understood through our intellect and the use of reason. It is our God-given instinct to be in right relationship with God, other people, the world, and ourselves. The basis for natural law is our participation in God's wisdom and goodness because we are created in the divine likeness. *(page 54)*

nuptial Something related to marriage or a marriage ceremony. *(page 63)*

P

Paschal Mystery The work of salvation accomplished by Jesus Christ mainly through his Passion, death, Resurrection, and Ascension. *(page 23)*

Pharisees A Jewish sect at the time of Jesus known for its strict adherence to the Law. *(page 62)*

presbyterate The name given to priests as a group, especially in a diocese; based on the Greek word *presbyter,* which means "elder." *(page 120)*

prophet A person God chooses to speak his message of salvation. In the Bible, primarily a communicator of a divine message of repentance to the Chosen People, not necessarily a person who predicted the future. *(page 44)*

providence The guidance, material goods, and care provided by God that is sufficient to meet our needs. *(page 191)*

R

religious communities A group of men or women religious who are joined by a common charism. *(page 174)*

S

sacred bond A binding commitment within the Church—especially to a particular state in life—that is recognized by Canon Law. Religious vows are considered sacred bonds, but a sacred bond does not necessarily need to be a religious vow. Other sacred bonds could include promises or oaths. *(page 179)*

Sacred Chrism Perfumed olive oil that has been consecrated. It is used for anointing in the Sacraments of Baptism, Confirmation, and Holy Orders. *(page 23)*

seminary A school established for the formation of future priests. *(page 135)*

spiritual director A priest or other person who is experienced and knowledgeable about faith, prayer, and spirituality and helps others to grow in their relationship with God. *(page 49)*

spiritual works of mercy Charitable actions that respond to people's spiritual needs and show respect for human dignity. The traditional list of seven works includes sharing knowledge, giving advice to those who need it, comforting those who suffer, being patient with others, forgiving those who hurt you, giving correction to those who need it, and praying for the living and the dead. *(page 162)*

successors A successor is a person who succeeds, or comes after, another as office holder. Bishops, led by the Pope, the Bishop of Rome, are the successors of the Apostles. *(page 109)*

T

Tradition This word (from the Latin, meaning "to hand on") refers to the process of passing on the Gospel message. Tradition, which began with the oral communication of the Gospel by the Apostles, was written down in Scripture, is handed down and lived out in the life of the Church, and is interpreted by the Magisterium under the guidance of the Holy Spirit. *(page 10)*

V

vocal prayer A prayer that is spoken aloud or silently, such as the Lord's Prayer. *(page 190)*

vocation A call from God to all members of the Church to embrace a life of holiness. Specifically, it refers to a call to live the holy life as an ordained minister, as a vowed religious (sister or brother), or in a Christian marriage. Single life that involves a personal consecration or commitment to a permanent, celibate gift of self to God and one's neighbor is also a vocational state. *(page 9)*

W

wisdom literature The Old Testament Books of Proverbs, Job, Ecclesiastes, Sirach, and the Wisdom of Solomon. *(page 57)*

Index
Page numbers in italics refer to illustrations.

G

Gabriel, 17–18
Genesis, 56–57
gift of self, 113–114
Gift of the Holy Spirit, 23
gifts, 24, 193
"giving the bride away," 78
Glenmary Home Missioners, 180
God
    communion with, 9, 10
    discernment and, 159–161
    heart and, 10, 15, 191–193
    Law of, 57, 61, 62, 93
    listening to, 194–197
    longing for, 10–11
    unity with, 154
    walking with, 198–207
    Where is he leading me?, 188–190
God's call
    holiness and, 9
    in the New Testament, 17–21
    in the Old Testament, 14–17
    response to, 26–37
    we are called by, 8–24
God's will, 150, 187–197, 200–203
Good Samaritan, 30
governing, 112
governments, 41, 43
grace
    Baptism and, 22
    commitments and, 151, 203
    consecrated life and, 157
    diaconate and, 126
    holiness and, 12, 24
    marriage and, 63
    rejecting, 202
    responsibility and, 203
    Sacrament of Holy Orders and, 142–143
    Sacrament of Matrimony and, 36, 86
    Sacraments and, 23
    vocations and, 9, 129
Great Commandment, 29, 31
Greeks, 10, 27
Gregory XI, 184

H

happiness, 12–13, 157–158, 203
healing, 123
heart, the, 10, 15, 191–193
Heaven, 9, 84, 150, 154–155, 156, 157
Hecker, Isaac Thomas, 180
Henry VIII, 89
hermits (eremitic life), 152, 170–173, 174, 184
Hinduism, 10
holiness. *see also* sanctifying
    consecrated life and, 149, 159–161
    Donatism and, 141
    everyday actions and, 156
    God's call and, 9
    grace and, 12, 24
    marriage and, 63, 86–87
    Sacraments and, 23
    universal call to, 12
Holy Communion, 23
Holy Family, 98
holy oils, 118, 119
Holy Orders. *see also* Sacrament of Holy Orders
    character and, 142
    qualifications for, 130–133
    Sacrament of, 129–144
    three degrees of, 115–127
Holy Sacrifice of the Mass, 113
Holy See, 140, 154
Holy Spirit
    Apostles and, 108–109
    bishops and, 111
    charisms and, 24
    Church and, 107, 154
    discernment and, 191
    Gift of the, 23
    holiness and, 12
    Sacrament of Holy Orders and, 142–143
    symbol of fire and, 204
    tradition and, 10
    witnessing and, 207
Holy Trinity, 23, 24, 33, 95, 191
homosexuality, 54
hope, 156, 157
Hosea, Book of, 59
humility, 149, 150
husbands, 73, 83

Acknowledgments

Scripture texts used in this work are taken from the *New American Bible, revised edition* © 2010, 1991, 1986, 1970 Confraternity of Christian Doctrine, Inc., Washington, D.C. All Rights Reserved. No part of this work may be reproduced or transmitted in any form or by any means, electronic or mechanical, including photocopying, recording, or by any information storage and retrieval system, without permission in writing from the copyright owner.

The excerpts labeled *Catechism* and *CCC* are from the English translation of the *Catechism of the Catholic Church* for use in the United States of America, second edition. Copyright © 1994 by the United States Catholic Conference, Inc.—Libreria Editrice Vaticana (LEV). English translation of the *Catechism of the Catholic Church: Modifications from the Editio Typica* copyright © 1997 by the United States Catholic Conference, Inc.—LEV.

The quotation on page 10 from *Declaration on the Relation of the Church to Non-Christian Religions* (*Nostra Aetate*, 1965), number 2; the quotation on page 12 from *Dogmatic Constitution on the Church* (*Lumen Gentium*, 1964), number 39; and the excerpt in the sidebar on page 55 from *Pastoral Constitution on the Church in the Modern World* (*Gaudium et Spes*, 1965), number 48; are from *Vatican Council II: Constitutions, Decrees, Declarations*, Austin Flannery, general editor (Northport, NY: Costello Publishing Company, 1996). Copyright © 1996 by Reverend Austin Flannery, OP.

The quotations in the sidebar on page 11 are from *Man's Search for Meaning*, by Viktor E. Frankl (New York: Simon and Schuster, 1985), pages 56–57 and 123. Copyright © 1959, 1962, 1984 by Victor E. Frankl.

The quotation in the sidebar on page 13 is from "Address of John Paul II to the Young People at the Kiel Center," number 4, at *www.vatican.va/holy_father/john_paul_ii/travels/documents/hf_jp-ii_spe_26011999_stlouis-youth_en.html*. Copyright © LEV.

The quotation on page 22 and the excerpt on page 95 from the English translation of *Rite of Baptism for Children* © 1969, International Commission on English in the Liturgy Corporation (ICEL), numbers 60 and 70; the quotations on pages 80–81 and 86; and the excerpt in the sidebar on page 81 from the English translation of *Rite of Marriage* © 1969 ICEL, numbers 24, 24, 25, 28, 25, and 33; and the prayer in the sidebar on page 157 from the English translation of *Order of Christian Funerals* © 1985, ICEL, number 72; are found in *The Rites of the Catholic Church*, volume one, prepared by the ICEL, a Joint Commission of Catholic Bishops'

Conferences (Collegeville, MN: Liturgical Press, 1990]. Copyright © 1990 by the Order of St. Benedict, Collegeville, MN. Used with permission of the ICEL.

The quotation on page 28 is from "Message of the Holy Father to the Youth of the World on the Occasion of the XII World Youth Day," number 3, at *www.vatican.va/holy_father/john_paul_ii/messages/youth/documents/hf_jp-ii_mes_15081996_xii-world-youth-day_en.html*. Copyright © LEV.

The quotation in the sidebar on page 33 is from *Story of a Soul: The Autobiography of Saint Thérèse of Lisieux*, translated from the original manuscripts by John Clark, third edition (Washington, DC: ICS Publications, 1996), pages 207 and 208. Copyright © Washington Province of Discalced Carmelites, 1975, 1976, 1996.

The excerpt on page 41 is from *From a Letter to Diognetus: The Christians in the World* at *www.vatican.va/spirit/documents/spirit_20010522_diogneto_en.html*.

The excerpt on page 49 is from *The Thrill of the Chaste: Finding Fulfillment While Keeping Your Clothes On*, by Dawn Eden (Nashville, TN: Thomas Nelson, 2006), page 22. Copyright © 2006 by Dawn Eden.

The excerpt in the sidebar on page 68 and the excerpt on page 97 are from *On the Role of the Christian Family in the Modern World* (*Familiaris Consortio*), numbers 17 and 6, at *www.vatican.va/holy_father/john_paul_ii/apost_exhortations/documents/hf_jp-ii_exh_19811122_familiaris-consortio_en.html*. Copyright © LEV.

The excerpt on page 98 is from "Angelus: Feast of the Holy Family," number 2, at *www.vatican.va/holy_father/john_paul_ii/angelus/2001/documents/hf_jp-ii_ang_20011230_en.html*. Copyright © LEV.

The excerpt in the sidebar on page 105 is from "Homily of His Holiness Benedict XVI," at *www.vatican.va/holy_father/benedict_xvi/homilies/2010/documents/hf_ben-xvi_hom_20100603_corpus-domini_en.html*. Copyright © 2010 LEV.

The quotation on page 106 from "Eucharistic Prayer I" is from the English translation of *The Roman Missal* © 2010, ICEL. All rights reserved. Used with permission of the ICEL.

The excerpt in the sidebar on page 109 and the prayer in the sidebar on page 139 are from the English translation of the *Rites of Ordination of a Bishop, of Priests, and of Deacons* (Second Typical Edition) © 2000, 2002, ICEL, numbers 83 and 135 (Washington, DC: USCCB, 2003). Copyright © 2003, USCCB, Washington, D.C. All rights reserved. No part of this work may be reproduced or transmitted in any form or by any means, electronic or mechanical, including photocopying, recording, or by any information storage and retrieval system, without permission in writing from the copyright holder. Used with permission of the ICEL.

The quotations in the sidebar on page 113 and on page 153 are from the *Code of Canon Law*, numbers 1752 and 573.2, at *www.vatican.va/ archive/ENG1104/_INDEX*. Copyright © LEV.

The excerpt in the sidebar on page 126 is from "Deacons Are Called to a Life of Holiness," at *www.vatican.va/holy_father/john_paul_ii/audiences/ alpha/data/aud19931020en.html*. Copyright © LEV.

The excerpt on page 131 is from *Declaration on the Question of Admission of Women to the Ministerial Priesthood (Inter Insigniores)* at *www.vatican.va/roman_curia/congregations/cfaith/documents/rc_con_ cfaith_doc_19761015_inter-insigniores_en.html*. Copyright © LEV.

The quotation on page 137 is from *Decree on Priestly Training (Optatam Totius)*, number 4, at *www.vatican.va/archive/hist_councils/ ii_vatican_council/documents/vat-ii_decree_19651028_optatam-totius_ en.html*. Copyright © LEV.

The excerpt in the sidebar on page 143 was written by John Cardinal O'Connor and appears in the introduction to *A Priest Forever: The Life of Father Eugene Hamilton*, by Fr. Benedict Groeschel (Huntington, IN: Our Sunday Visitor, 1998), page 9. Copyright © 1998 by Our Sunday Visitor Publishing Division, Our Sunday Visitor, Inc.

The excerpt in the sidebar on page 167 is from "Address of His Holiness Benedict XVI to the Participants in the International Congress— Pilgrimage of the *Ordo Virginum (The Order of Virgins)*, at *www.vatican. va/holy_father/benedict_xvi/speeches/2008/may/documents/hf_ben-xvi_ spe_20080515_ordo-virginum_en.html*. Copyright © 2008 LEV.

The quotation on pages 169–170 is from the English translation of *Rite of Consecration to a Life of Virginity* © 1975, ICEL, number 2, in *The Rites of the Catholic Church*, volume two, prepared by the ICEL, a Joint Commission of Catholic Bishops' Conferences (Collegeville, MN: Liturgical Press, 1991). Copyright © 1991, the Order of St. Benedict, Collegeville, MN. Used with permission of the ICEL.

The excerpt in the sidebar on page 199 is from "Apostolic Journey to Madrid on the Occasion of the 26th World Youth Day, August 18, 2011: Words of the Holy Father at the Beginning of the Eucharist Celebration," at *www.vatican.va/holy_father/benedict_xvi/homilies/2011/documents/ hf_ben-xvi_hom_20110821_xxvi-gmg-madrid_en.html*. Copyright © 2011 LEV.

To view copyright terms and conditions for Internet materials cited here, log on to the home pages for the referenced Web sites.

During this book's preparation, all citations, facts, figures, names, addresses, telephone numbers, Internet URLs, and other pieces of information cited within were verified for accuracy. The authors and Saint Mary's Press staff have made every attempt to reference current and valid sources, but we cannot guarantee the content of any source, and we are not responsible for any changes that may have occurred since our verification. If you find an error in, or have a question or concern about, any of the information or sources listed within, please contact Saint Mary's Press.

Endnotes Cited in Quotations from the *Catechism of the Catholic Church*, Second Edition

Section 3
1. *Roman Pontifical,* Ordination of Bishops 26, Prayer of Consecration.
2. *Roman Pontifical,* Ordination of Priests 22, Prayer of Consecration.
3. *Roman Pontifical,* Ordination of Deacons 21, Prayer of Consecration.
4. Byzantine Liturgy, *Euchologion.*